Did Jesus Really Rise
from the Dead?

Did Jesus Really Rise from the Dead?

Questions and Answers about the Life, Death, and Resurrection of Jesus Christ

Carl E. Olson

Ignatius Press–Augustine Institute

San Francisco Greenwood Village, CO

Ignatius Press Distribution
P.O. Box 1339
Fort Collins, CO 80522
Tel: (800) 651-1531
www.ignatius.com

Augustine Institute
6160 S. Syracuse Way, Suite 310
Greenwood Village, CO 80111
Tel: (866) 767-3155
www.augustineinstitute.org

Cover Design: Jessica Hallman

Cover Art: *Empty Tomb*, © Kevron2001, Adobe Stock

Contents

Introduction

From the start, the proclamation of the Resurrection of Jesus Christ from the dead has been met with a wide range of emotions and responses: fear, amazement, joy, perplexity, astonishment—and disbelief. In the succinct account at the end of the Gospel of Mark, the three women, Mary Magdalene, Mary the mother of James, and Salome, who go to anoint Jesus's body with spices were amazed to find a young man in white robes, an angel, sitting in an otherwise empty tomb. "Do not be amazed," he told them, "you seek Jesus of Nazareth, who was crucified. He has risen, he is not here; see the place where they laid him" (Mk 16:6). The women fled the tomb, trembling and astonished, "and they said nothing to any one, for they were afraid" (Mk 16:8).

So afraid, we read, that they said nothing to anyone. Who would believe them? Why would anyone believe them? And, sure enough, when Mary Magdalene told the grieving disciples that Jesus had appeared to her the following morning, "they would not believe it" (Mk 16:11). In the words of Luke, the account given "seemed to them an idle tale, and they did not believe them" (Lk 24:11). "For the early Christians," writes noted New Testament scholar Craig S. Keener, "neither the empty tomb nor the testimony of the women was adequate evidence by itself (*cf.* Lk 24:22–24); they also depended on the testimony of the men for the public forum (*cf.* 1 Cor 15:5–8)." The disbelief of the male disciples is, by any measure, both understandable and embarrassing, and Keener states that the "criterion of embarrassment indicates that no one had apologetic reason to invent the testimony of these women."[1]

The most famous story of early disbelief, of course, is John's account of "doubting Thomas":

> So the other disciples told him, "We have seen the Lord." But he said to them, "Unless I see in his hands the print of the nails, and place my finger in the mark of the nails, and place my hand in his side, I will not believe." (Jn 20:25)

There has been much commentary on this story, but the point here is simply that from the beginning—that is, from the moment that something happened in the tomb in the Garden—there has been disbelief, even among those who lived and walked with Jesus. Further, the early Christians did not apparently spend time proclaiming first and foremost the teachings and parables of Jesus, but rather focused on his rising from the dead. And, again, it's noteworthy how often this message was not only rejected but inspired scorn, disdain, and even persecution.

Peter, in his sermon at Pentecost, stated:

> "Men of Israel, hear these words: Jesus of Nazareth, a man attested to you by God with mighty works and wonders and signs which God did through him in your midst, as you yourselves know—this Jesus, delivered up according to the definite plan and foreknowledge of God, you crucified and killed by the hands of lawless men. But God raised him up, having loosed the pangs of death, because it was not possible for him to be held by it." (Acts 2:22–24; *cf.* 2:27, 31)

---

[1]   Craig S. Keener, *The Historical Jesus of the Gospels* (Grand Rapids, MI: William B. Eerdmans Publishing Company, 2009), 331.

This was not just part of a rather sophisticated theological argument for Jesus's messianic identity and divine nature but was at the very center of that argument, as emphasized by the head Apostle: "This Jesus God raised up, and of that we all are witnesses" (Acts 2:32). Not too many days later, Peter addressed a group of people gathered near the Temple and repeated similar words: "But you denied the Holy and Righteous One, and asked for a murderer to be granted to you, and killed the Author of life, whom God raised from the dead. To this we are witnesses" (Acts 3:14–15).

As we will see, *witness*—*martyria* in the Greek (from which comes the word "martyr")—and *testimony*[2] are important terms for the authors of the New Testament books. This is especially true for John, who uses the word twenty-six times in his Gospel (it also appears seven times in the Synoptic Gospels and six times in the Book of Revelation). Peter, at the start of his first epistle, emphasizes the "living hope" the early Christians held on to "through the resurrection of Jesus Christ from the dead" (1 Pet 1:3), and later situates his authority, at least in part, on being "a witness of the sufferings of Christ as well as a partaker in the glory that is to

---

[2] "I suggest that we need to recover the sense in which the Gospels are testimony," writes the noted New Testament scholar Richard Bauckham. "This does not mean that they are testimony rather than history. It means that the histiography they are is testimony.... Trusting testimony is not an irrational act of faith that leaves critical rationality aside; it is, on the contrary, the rationally appropriate way of responding to authentic testimony. Gospels understood as testimony are the entirely appropriate means of access to the historical reality of Jesus" (*Jesus and the Eyewitnesses: The Gospels as Eyewitness Testimony* [Grand Rapids, MI: William B. Eerdmans Publishing Company, 2006], 5). Bauckham adds: "But it is also a rather neglected fact that all history, like all knowledge, relies on testimony." This and related points will be addressed in detail later in this book.

be revealed" (1 Pet 5:1). The significance of being a witness to the Resurrection is highlighted at the beginning of the Acts of the Apostles, as the Eleven go about choosing a replacement for Judas:

> So one of the men who have accompanied us during all the time that the Lord Jesus went in and out among us, beginning from the baptism of John until the day when he was taken up from us—one of these men must become with us a witness to his resurrection. (Acts 1:21–22)

But, again, not everyone accepted the witness of the Apostles. While Luke, in Acts of the Apostles, emphasizes the growth and expansion of the early Church (*cf.* Acts 2:47, 4:4, 6:1, 7, 11:21, 16:5), he also depicts both Jews and Greeks rejecting the message preached by the Apostles precisely because of the Resurrection. The priests and the Sadducees "came upon them, annoyed because they were teaching the people and proclaiming in Jesus the resurrection from the dead" (Acts 4:1–2). In Paul's address to the Athenians at the Areopagus (or Mars Hill), which was a place for juridical deliberation and philosophical debate, the point of division was not the existence or nature of God or points of morality but the Christian belief in Jesus's victory over death. Paul says,

> "because he [God] has fixed a day on which he will judge the world in righteousness by a man whom he has appointed, and of this he has given assurance to all men by raising him from the dead."
>
> Now when they heard of the resurrection of the dead, some mocked; but others said, "We will hear you again about this." (Acts 17:31–32)

And it is Paul who put the matter in stark relief, telling the Christians in Corinth that what he preached and what they believed was centered squarely on the Resurrection—and doing so, it seems, because of a failure of some to believe such an event was real:

> Whether then it was I or they, so we preach and so you believed. Now if Christ is preached as raised from the dead, how can some of you say that there is no resurrection of the dead? But if there is no resurrection of the dead, then Christ has not been raised; if Christ has not been raised, then our preaching is in vain and your faith is in vain. We are even found to be misrepresenting God, because we testified of God that he raised Christ, whom he did not raise if it is true that the dead are not raised. For if the dead are not raised, then Christ has not been raised. If Christ has not been raised, your faith is futile and you are still in your sins. (1 Cor 15:11–17)

In the words of Pope Benedict XVI, in his second book on Jesus of Nazareth: "The Christian faith stands or falls with the truth of the testimony that Christ is risen from the dead."[3] The Resurrection of the Christ is, to put it simply, *the event* that divides. And today, some 2,000 years after Christ walked the earth, it divides in at least three important ways.

The Historical Jesus and the Christ of Faith

First, belief in the Resurrection is, for many people today, the line that divides Jesus the Man—sometimes called the "historical Jesus" or "historical Christ"—from Jesus Christ the God-man, the Incarnate Word, the risen Lord. "For many minds," wrote the French theologian Jean Daniélou over fifty years ago, "the Resurrection of Christ represents the point at which they stop short. Up to the time of His Passion Christ is a historical figure. From the Resurrection onward, He

---

[3] Benedict XVI, *Jesus of Nazareth—Holy Week: From the Entrance into Jerusalem to the Resurrection* (San Francisco: Ignatius Press, 2011), 241.

belongs to the realm of faith."[4] While relatively few skeptics deny outright that Jesus existed, they earn their skeptical stripes by denying that he rose from the dead.

An interesting example of this is found in the writing of the prolific scholar Bart D. Ehrman, professor at University of North Carolina and author of over two dozen books, both academic and popular, about the Bible and Jesus. Ehrman's recent book *Did Jesus Exist?* takes on "mythicists"—those who deny that Jesus was a real, historical figure. Ehrman, in a Huffington Post essay about his book, likens such mythicists to those who deny the Holocaust, observing that this "unusually vociferous group of nay-sayers maintains that Jesus is a myth invented for nefarious (or altruistic) purposes by the early Christians who modeled their savior along the lines of pagan divine men who, it is alleged, were also born of a virgin on Dec. 25, who also did miracles, who also died as an atonement for sin and were then raised from the dead."[5] He notes that few of these mythicists have any training "in ancient history, religion, biblical studies or any cognate field," and no mythicists teaches New Testament of early Christianity at "any accredited institution of higher learning in the Western world."[6] Why? Because belief that Jesus didn't exist is simply "so extreme and so unconvincing to 99.99% of the real experts"[7] that they don't qualify for such academic posts.

---

4   Jean Daniélou, *Christ and Us* (New York: Sheed and Ward, 1961), 142.
5   Bart D. Ehrman, "Did Jesus Exist," *The Huffington Post*, March 20, 2012, http://www.huffingtonpost.com/bart-d-ehrman/did-jesus-exist_b_1349544.html.
6   Ibid.
7   Ibid.

However, Ehrman admits that the mythicist movement is growing and is gaining confidence. He doesn't name names, but a leading mythicist is Richard Dawkins, famed English evolutionary biologist, leading atheist, and author of the 2006 best-selling book *The God Delusion*.[8] In that book Dawkins took up the mythicist line with great vigor, if not a corresponding intellectual rigor, blithely dismissing what he calls the "Jesus legend."

"The nineteenth century," wrote Dawkins, "is the last time when it was possible for an educated person to admit to believing in miracles like the virgin birth without embarrassment. When pressed, many educated Christians today are too loyal to deny the virgin birth and the resurrection. But it embarrasses them because their rational minds know it is absurd, so they would much rather not be asked."[9] Every supposedly distinctive feature of the life of Christ—including the Resurrection—is, Dawkins insists, simply stolen from already existing religions in the Mediterranean world and the Near East.

The roots of this approach—which is featured and touted on numerous websites run by skeptics, atheists, and conspiracy theorists—go back to the eighteenth century, when Charles François Dupuis (1742–1809) wrote *The Origin of All Religious Worship,* one of the first-known attempts to show that all religions, including Christianity, are essentially the same and that Jesus was the mythical creation of early Christians drawing upon various pagan myths. This gained currency in the United States in the late 1800s with the publication of

---

[8]   Richard Dawkins, *The God Delusion* (Boston: Houghton Mifflin, 2006).

[9]   Ibid., 187.

The World's Sixteen Crucified Saviors (or *Christianity Before Christ*), written in 1875 by Kersey Graves (1813–83). Jesus, the book asserted, was not an actual person, but a creation based on earlier stories of deities or god-men saviors who had been crucified and descended to and ascended from the underworld. Graves, who was born into a Quaker family, was an atheist who employed spiritualism in order to gain insights into historical events and personages.

Ehrman, who rejected the Christianity of his youth and early adulthood to become a self-professed agnostic, points out that the sort of "alleged parallels between Jesus and the 'pagan' savior-gods" peddled by Graves and his disciples are simply nonsense and "in most instances reside in the modern imagination."[10] While Ehrman thinks the Gospels "are riddled with problems"—in part because of "biased authors"—he correctly notes that "historians can never dismiss sources simply because they are biased."[11] There are, in fact, many sources for the life of Christ, argues Ehrman, the number of which is "pretty astounding for an ancient figure of any kind."[12] After touching on some other reasons for the historical veracity of Jesus's existence, Ehrman concludes: "Whether we like it or not, Jesus certainly existed."[13]

Flash forward to Ehrman's 2015 book *How Jesus Became God: The Exaltation of a Jewish Preacher from Galilee*,[14] an extended argument that the supernatural characteristics of Jesus's person and life were superimposed—as the subtitle

---

[10]   Bart D. Ehrman, "Did Jesus Exist?"
[11]   Ibid.
[12]   Ibid.
[13]   Ibid.
[14]   Bart D. Ehrman, *How Jesus Became God: The Exaltation of a Jewish Preacher from Galilee* (New York: HarperOne, 2015), Kindle eBook.

suggests—upon a very mortal "apocalyptic prophet who was anticipating that God was soon to intervene in human affairs to overthrow the forces of evil and set up a good kingdom here on earth."[15] This message was not unique to Jesus, says Ehrman; rather, the uniqueness of Jesus is found elsewhere: "Belief in the resurrection is what eventually led his followers to claim that Jesus was God."[16]

Note that Ehrman references *belief* in the Resurrection—not the Resurrection itself. Put simply, Ehrman argues that we cannot know, from historical study, that Jesus was really raised from the dead. "I argue," he writes, "that when it comes to miracles such as the resurrection, historical sciences simply are of no help in establishing what happened."[17] In other words, faith and historical facts have, at best, an uneasy relationship; they are "two very different ways of 'knowing.'"[18] As a historian, Ehrman insists that Jesus really did exist. And, as a historian, he further insists we cannot know if the Resurrection actually happened.[19]

Is Ehrman correct? Is the Resurrection completely beyond the grasp of historical fact and knowledge? Must belief in the Resurrection be left only to the realm of faith? What sort of historical evidence is "fact" and how can we tell? These and related questions will be taken up in the chapters that follow.

---

[15] Ibid., location 1922.
[16] Ibid., location 1956.
[17] Ibid.
[18] Ibid.
[19] For a detailed critique of Ehrman's book, see *How God Became Jesus: The Real Origins of Belief in Jesus' Divine Nature* (Grand Rapids, MI: Zondervan, 2014), written by five Evangelical scholars.

Orthodoxy versus Heresy

The second line is closely related to the first, in part because it also relies on the modern distinction between the "historical Jesus" and the "Christ of faith." It is the line between orthodox Christianity and what might be called a "new Christianity": a spirituality that rejects traditional beliefs and historical expressions of the Christian faith while reinterpreting those beliefs and expressions in radical ways. A good example of this "new" form of Christianity is retired Episcopal bishop John Shelby Spong (b. 1931), who is the author of books such as *Living in Sin? A Bishop Rethinks Human Sexuality*, *Rescuing the Bible from Fundamentalism: A Bishop Rethinks the Meaning of Scripture*, *Born of a Woman: A Bishop Rethinks the Birth of Jesus*, *Eternal Life: A New Vision: Beyond Religion, Beyond Theism, Beyond Heaven and Hell*, and *Resurrection: Myth or Reality? A Bishop's Search for the Origins of Christianity*. As those titles indicate, Spong's ambition is to rethink and remake the central doctrines of Christianity: the nature of God, the Incarnation, the Resurrection, and salvation and judgment.

In his more recent book *Jesus for the Non-Religious*, Spong has a chapter called, "The Eternal Truth Inside the Myths of the Resurrection and Ascension." Spong argues that when "we go to the details of the resurrection as found in the gospels, we are confronted with a host of assertions that are contradictory, confusing and baffling."[20] The physicality of Jesus's Resurrection, he insists, is something that was added many decades after the death of Jesus, when a "quite obviously late-developing tradition would literally overwhelm the early

---

[20] John Shelby Spong, *Jesus for the Non-Religious* (New York: HarperCollins, 2007), 119.

nonphysical tradition and begin to form the now common understanding of Easter."[21] He later states, emphatically:

> The resurrection language of the gospels is literal nonsense. . . . A resuscitated Jesus does not walk out of his tomb in some physical form that can eat, drink, walk, talk, teach and expound on scriptures. This "raised" bodily person does not appear and disappear at will, walk through walls, or invite the doubters to feel his wounds. . . . All of these things are interpretive tales employed in the process of human explanation in which a life-changing inner experience was enabled to be communicated in the language of history by the use of external symbols.[22]

Spong admits, even insists, that something "moving and profound" happened "at the central moment in the Christian story," but that it is a mistake to "literalize Easter."[23] In fact, he claims that such a literalizing error "has become the definitive heresy of traditional Protestant and Catholic Christianity."[24] No one, Spong says repeatedly and in different ways, who is truly modern and enlightened can accept as literally true the central beliefs of orthodox, traditional Christianity, including the Resurrection. Spong waxes in a somewhat condescending fashion that the Resurrection, and indeed the entire "Jesus story," is an "invitation to journey beyond human limits, beyond human boundaries, into the realm of that experience that we call God."[25] He is less ambiguous in later claiming that nearly every detail of Jesus's life as recorded in the Gospels—his conception, birth, ministry, teaching, suffering, Death, Resurrection, and Ascension—are fabricated, created

---

[21] Ibid.
[22] Ibid., 122–23.
[23] Ibid., 127.
[24] Ibid.
[25] Ibid.

by the early Christians who used those details and events out of necessity. Now, Spong asserts, they are no longer needed; we need a completely new way of understanding Jesus. And this means interpreting the Resurrection as a spiritual event that cannot be summed up or captured by "creedal or doctrinal formulas."[26]

Spong repeatedly refers to "mystery" while rejecting just about every historical detail about Jesus. "I seek," he explains, "a Jesus beyond scripture, beyond creeds, beyond doctrines, beyond dogmas and beyond religion itself."[27] The mystery, then, is this: why bother? Why should anyone bother with such a Jesus? Especially when Jesus "is not an end in himself, as Christians have so mistakenly assumed," as Spong insists, "Jesus is but a doorway into the wonder of God."[28] Could it be that Christians really have been so mistaken about the Gospels and the truth about Jesus for twenty centuries? Should the Resurrection, along with other events in the life of Christ, be understood as spiritual or metaphorical events that do not reflect what really happened in the material, temporal realm? Is it accurate to say that modern and post-modern people of the twenty-first century cannot and should not be asked to believe such accounts?

Spong's approach, while extreme to the point of not being Christian in any sense of the term, certainly appeals to a culture that increasingly embraces an individualistic "spiritual but not religious" approach to matters of faith and morality. (It should come as no surprise that Spong finds traditional Christianity to be sexist and homophobic.) It also

---

[26] Ibid., 135.
[27] Ibid., 137.
[28] Ibid.

resonates among those who, for various reasons, think the Church's doctrines and creeds to be too rigid and assertive; in short, it allows people to hold on to a skeleton of familiar language while fleshing it out with their own subjective needs or emotional desires. Christianity without the Resurrection is a variation of Christianity without the Cross—a path to "enlightenment" that ends up being remarkably self-assuring and self-absorbed.

Put another way, how is Spong's mystical dismissal of the historical foundations of Christianity any different from the neo-Hindu monism for the masses peddled by the prolific New Age author Deepak Chopra?[29] In his 2008 best-selling book *Third Jesus: The Christ We Cannot Ignore,* the former medical doctor teaches that "what made Jesus the Son of God was the fact that he had achieved God-consciousness"[30] and that "Jesus intended to save the world by showing others the path to God-consciousness."[31] To that end, Chopra posits three versions of Jesus: two false and one true. The "first" Jesus "is historical and we know next to nothing about him."[32] Chopra employs contradictions in striving to do away with this Jesus. For example: "The first Jesus was a rabbi who wandered the shores of northern Galilee many centuries ago. This Jesus still feels close enough to touch." And yet, while he seems so close and knowable, he is completely unknowable.

---

[29] Parts of this section are adapted from my essay "Chopra's Christ: The Mythical Creation of a New Age Panthevangelist," *Ignatius Insight,* May 5, 2008, http://www.ignatiusinsight.com/features2008/colson_chopra_may08.asp.

[30] Deepak Chopra, *Third Jesus: The Christ We Cannot Ignore* (New York: Harmony Books, 2008), 3–4.

[31] Ibid., 10.

[32] Ibid., 8.

Why? "This historical Jesus has been lost, however, swept away by history."[33]

Then, over two hundred pages later, Chopra muses, "History may blur Jesus' biography, but it can't put out the light."[34] So, which is it: swept away or merely blurred? Chopra's argument—using the term with deliberate looseness—is that "the first Jesus is less than consistent, as a closer reading of the gospels will show."[35] He is either unaware or dismissive of the fact that Christians have long grappled with the "baffling contradictions"[36] personified by Jesus, and have concluded—to put it succinctly—that if we could fully understand everything about Jesus, it would strongly suggest he was not divine at all. Chopra, however, cannot be bothered by the study and writings of Christian theologians and scholars. He is far more interested in casting aside what he calls the "second" Jesus, who is "the Jesus built up over thousands of years by theologians and other scholars."[37] (In fact, Chopra never quotes any reputable Christian theologian or mentions traditional Christian arguments.) This "second" Jesus, Chopra flatly states, "never existed" and "doesn't even lay claim to the fleeting substance of the first Jesus."[38] At this point Chopra provides some comic relief, saying that this supposedly non-existent Jesus created by the Church "is the Holy Ghost, the Three-in-One Christ, the source of sacraments and prayers that were unknown to the rabbi Jesus when he

---

[33] Ibid.
[34] Ibid., 217.
[35] Ibid., 8.
[36] Ibid.
[37] Ibid., 9.
[38] Ibid.

walked the earth."[39] Some questions come immediately to mind: If the historical Jesus has been "swept away by history" (just three paragraphs earlier!), how do we know what was known or unknown to him? Where does the Catholic Church teach that Jesus is the Holy Spirit? What does Chopra mean by "Three-in-One Christ"? Is he referring to the Trinity? Has he read even one basic manual of Christian theology?

The inconsistencies never let up. Chopra praises "the simplicity of Jesus' words" and then later writes, "Anyone can devise a new interpretation of the New Testament. Unfortunately, this great text is ambiguous and confusing enough to support almost any thesis about its meaning."[40] His open disdain for theology—from the Greek words *theos* (God) and *logia* (discourse or discussion)—seems simple enough: he doesn't like thinking logically about God or at least the personal God of the Jews and the Christians. And when Chopra encounters an argument or position he disagrees with, he simply dismisses it: "Theology is arbitrary; it can tell any story it wants, find any hidden meaning."[41] Chopra's own arbitrary methods and findings are apparently exempt from any such criticism.

The "third" Jesus, or Chopra's Christ, is remarkably similar to Spong's customized Jesus. The "third" Jesus is the Jesus who "taught his followers how to reach God-consciousness."[42] This Jesus was "a savior," but "not the savior, not the one and only Son of God. Rather, Jesus embodied the highest level of enlightenment. . . . Jesus intended to save the world by

---

[39] Ibid.
[40] Ibid., 139.
[41] Ibid., 136.
[42] Ibid., 9.

showing others the path to God-consciousness."[43] Then, having already claimed that the historical Jesus cannot be known and that the second Jesus is a nasty lie, Chopra offers an unconvincing olive branch: "Such a reading of the New Testament doesn't diminish the first two Jesuses. Rather, they are brought into sharper focus. In place of lost history and complex history, the third Jesus offers a direct relationship that is personal and present."[44] But if the historical Jesus cannot be known and the Jesus of doctrine and theology is a fabrication, how can they be "brought into sharper focus"?

What is notable here is that while Spong goes to great lengths to reinterpret the Resurrection, Chopra has little interest in what Christians have always understood to be the heart of the Gospels: the Passion, Death, and Resurrection of Jesus Christ. He makes the strange remark that "with the resurrection a flesh-and-blood man was transformed into completely divine substance—the Holy Spirit,"[45] and implies that the early Christians, desperate to have Jesus back with them, created the belief in the Resurrection[46]—echoing what both atheists and some liberal theologians also assert. Otherwise, nothing. There is much talk of Jesus pointing man toward "the divine" and "God-consciousness," but it is invariably ephemeral and vague. Reading Chopra trying to explain the nature of Jesus's life, work, Death, and Resurrection is like watching a madman shooting fog with a shotgun. He claims to have hit the target every time, but the fog remains and nothing has really happened, even while the shooter's cockiness grows with every blast.

---

43 Ibid., 10.
44 Ibid.
45 Ibid., 136.
46 Ibid., 179.

But Spong and Chopra do share the belief that Christianity is too literal, too earthly-minded, too rational, and too focused on Jesus as a unique figure. Chopra denounces the "abstract theological creation"[47] of the second Jesus—that is, the Jesus of traditional Christian belief and devotion—but, later denounces Christians for doing otherwise: "Christianity has done everything possible to humanize Jesus, for we cannot conceive of someone so completely transcendent that even our most cherished qualities, such as love and compassion, fall short of his reality."[48] There is a startling irony here, for many atheists dismiss Christianity as being far too mystical in nature, too heavenly-minded, too obsessed with the supernatural, and irrationally fixated on Jesus's being divine. And both groups paint traditional Christians as fundamentalist, hypocritical, rigid, hateful, and narrow-minded. Such Christians, Chopra opines, are so filled with "fundamentalist zeal" that they have "fallen back on the medieval tradition of Imitatio Christi, worshipping Christ by imitating him."[49] That's right—the evil forces of Christian fundamentalism are rooted in people seeking to both worship and imitate Jesus!

An essential message of *The Third Jesus* is the tired but popular mantra: spirituality is good, religion is bad (as in, "I'm spiritual, not religious!"). We need, Chopra exhorts readers, to discard "the model of religion. To gather together on the path isn't the same as forming a sect. There is no need for dogma, prayer, ritual, priests, or official scripture. No one is to be elevated above the rest."[50] However, Chopra's book, like Spong's books, is nothing if not dogmatic and authoritative

---

[47] Ibid., 9.
[48] Ibid., 220.
[49] Ibid., 222.
[50] Ibid., 171.

in tone and character. More importantly for the purpose of this book, Chopra fails to engage with the evidence and arguments that exist for the veracity of the Gospels in general and the Resurrection in particular. So, the line here is between those Christians who would defend—using reason, facts, history, and logic—the traditional belief in the Resurrection, and those who would either radically reinterpret or simply cast aside that belief.

Christianity, the Resurrection, and the Religions

"For quite a while now," laments theologian Gerhard Lohfink in his book *No Irrelevant Jesus,*

> many neopagans and quite a few of the baptized have been making up their own religions: they cobble together a private faith out of mismatched bits of the widest variety of religions and worldviews, because the church has scarcely anything to say to them or is simply irritating. Even among some "confessing" Christians, faith in central parts of the creed is gradually fading—the resurrection of the dead, for example. A good many orient themselves to foreign beliefs such as Buddhism or nature religions, or they make up their own mixture altogether.[51]

Lohfink says that amid such confusion "it is the church's urgent and even essential duty to make clear what is specifically Christian."[52] Such a task is difficult, in part because the Enlightenment project has aided and even promoted a dismissal of religious belief and has also encouraged a reactionary syncretism in which an often irrational stew of religion and spirituality is set up against the rather cold and rational

---

[51] Gerhard Lohfink, *No Irrelevant Jesus: On Jesus and the Church Today* (Collegeville, MN: Liturgical Press, 2014), 247. From the chapter titled "What Distinguishes Christianity from the Religions."

[52] Ibid., 248.

forces of scientism and technocracy. Thus, to put it simply, Christianity has been attacked from one side as superstitious and anti-reason and from the other as too exclusive and dogmatic, and thus fundamentalist. Joseph Cardinal Ratzinger, in a remarkable homily given at the Mass prior to the papal conclave in which he was elected pope, asked, "How many winds of doctrine have we known in recent decades, how many ideological currents, how many ways of thinking"?[53]

> The small boat of the thought of many Christians has often been tossed about by these waves—flung from one extreme to another: from Marxism to liberalism, even to libertinism; from collectivism to radical individualism; from atheism to a vague religious mysticism; from agnosticism to syncretism and so forth. Every day new sects spring up, and what St. Paul says about human deception and the trickery that strives to entice people into error (*cf.* Eph 4:14) comes true.
>
> Today, having a clear faith based on the Creed of the Church is often labeled as fundamentalism. Whereas relativism, that is, letting oneself be "tossed here and there, carried about by every wind of doctrine," seems the only attitude that can cope with modern times. We are building a dictatorship of relativism that does not recognize anything as definitive and whose ultimate goal consists solely of one's own ego and desires.
>
> We, however, have a different goal: the Son of God, the true man. He is the measure of true humanism.[54]

The *Catechism of the Catholic Church*, which then-Cardinal Ratzinger co-edited, states: "Belief in the resurrection of the dead has been an essential element of the Christian faith from

---

[53] Joseph Cardinal Ratzinger, "Homily of Joseph Cardinal Ratzinger, Dean of the College of Cardinals, Mass for the Election of the Supreme Pontiff, St. Peter's Basilica" (Vatican City: Libreria Editrice Vaticana, April 18, 2005), http://www.vatican.va/gpII/documents/homily-pro-eligendo-pontifice_20050418_en.html.

[54] Ibid.

its beginnings.... From the beginning, Christian faith in the resurrection has met with incomprehension and opposition (cf. Acts 17:32; 1 Cor 15:12–13). On no point does the Christian faith encounter more opposition than on the resurrection of the body (cf. St. Augustine, *En. in Ps.* 88,5:PL 37,1134)."[55] That was the case at the beginning, it is the case today, and it will be so until the end of time. As Lohfink discusses, the uniqueness of Christianity is found in its understanding of God (who is Creator, Personal, Triune), its belief that God became man and dwelt among us (the Incarnation), and its proclamation that through the Death and Resurrection of Jesus Christ, mankind can now have eternal, life-giving communion with God the Creator and Father. In the words of the *Catechism*:

> The Paschal mystery has two aspects: by his death, Christ liberates us from sin; by his Resurrection, he opens for us the way to a new life. This new life is above all justification that reinstates us in God's grace, "so that as Christ was raised from the dead by the glory of the Father, we too might walk in newness of life" (Rom 6:4; cf. 4:25). Justification consists in both victory over the death caused by sin and a new participation in grace (cf. Eph 2:4-5; 1 Pet 1:3). It brings about filial adoption so that men become Christ's brethren, as Jesus himself called his disciples after his Resurrection: "Go and tell my brethren" (Mt 28:10; Jn 20:17). We are brethren not by nature, but by the gift of grace, because that adoptive filiation gains us a real share in the life of the only Son, which was fully revealed in his Resurrection.[56]

This is unique to Christianity; no other religion holds to the same combined understanding of God, Jesus Christ, man, and salvation. And the Resurrection is essential to this

---

[55] *Catechism of the Catholic Church (CCC)*, 991, 996.
[56] *CCC*, 654.

radical understanding of reality. This is why the Apostle Paul told the Corinthians, "For I delivered to you as of first importance what I also received, that Christ died for our sins in accordance with the Scriptures, and that he was buried, and that he was raised on the third day in accordance with the Scriptures" (1 Cor 15:3–4).

Pope Benedict XVI, in *Jesus of Nazareth: The Infancy Narratives*, refers to the Protestant theologian Karl Barth's observation that "there are two moments in the story of Jesus when God intervenes directly in the material world: the virgin birth and the resurrection from the tomb, in which Jesus did not remain, nor see corruption."[57] Benedict states: "These two moments are a scandal to the modern spirit." Why? Because the modern mind and spirit, while God is "allowed" to "act in ideas and thoughts, in the spiritual domain—but not in the material. That is shocking. He does not belong there."[58] But that, Benedict further notes, "is precisely the point: God is God and he does not operate merely on the level of ideas."[59]

That is a direct rebuttal to the agnosticism of Bart Ehrman, the pseudo-Christianity of John Shelby Spong, and the New Age monism of Deepak Chopra. It also highlights that what is at stake in studying the Resurrection is not just the identity and divinity of Jesus Christ but also the nature of God and the purpose of creation and salvation history. In the pages that follow we will take up the question, "Did Jesus really rise from the dead?" while also touching on a number of closely related points.

---

[57] Benedict XVI, *Jesus of Nazareth: The Infancy Narratives* (New York: Random House, 2012), 56.
[58] Ibid.
[59] Ibid., 56–57.

In recent years there have been several excellent books, many of them more academic and scholarly in nature, written about the Resurrection,[60] along with more popular books that take up the same topic within the broader scope of the Gospels and the life of Christ. This book is not academic, but aims to draw upon academic works and scholarly studies while addressing, in question-and-answer format, the most fundamental questions and issues in a way that is accessible to a wide range of readers.

---

[60] Including *The Resurrection of the Son of God* (Minneapolis: Fortress Press, 2003) by N. T. Wright; *The Resurrection: An Interdisciplinary Symposium on the Resurrection of Jesus* (New York: Oxford University Press, 1998), edited by Stephen Davis, Daniel Kendall, SJ, and Gerald O'Collins, SJ; *Assessing the New Testament Evidence for the Historicity of the Resurrection of Jesus (Studies in the Bible and Early Christianity)* (Lewiston, NY: Edwin Mellen Press, 1989) by William Lane Craig; and *The Resurrection of Jesus: A New Historiographical Approach* (Downers Grove, IL: IVP Academic, 2010) by Michael R. Licona.

CHAPTER 1

What's the Point?

Q. You appeared, in your Introduction, to be rather dismissive of those skeptics or atheists who argue that Jesus never existed and that the gospels of Matthew, Mark, Luke, and John cannot be taken seriously as works of history. But aren't those the sort of people who tend to get more attention than scholars?

It's a fair question and one that will, in fact, be addressed throughout this book directly and indirectly, precisely because it's impossible to say the Resurrection of Christ really happened if Jesus never existed, and because belief in that event is deeply and directly connected to the historical accuracy and veracity of the Gospels and the rest of the New Testament. And so, many points and specifics will be considered in the pages ahead.

That said, let's consider a couple of those points right at the start. We saw in the Introduction that Bart Ehrman, the author of many academic and popular books about Jesus and the New Testament (and a self-described agnostic), dismissed those "mythicists" who claim that Jesus is a mythological figure created out of thin air. He did this in part because the quality and quantity of historical sources for the life of Christ are "pretty astounding for an ancient figure of any kind."[1]

---

[1]   Ehrman, "Did Jesus Really Exist?"

While Ehrman, a skeptical scholar, is astounded by the wealth of ancient documentation, the late Christopher Hitchens, a rather sneering atheist, expressed astonishment in *God Is Not Great: How Religion Poisons Everything*[2] that Ehrman had somewhere noted "that the account of Jesus' resurrection in the Gospel of Mark was only added many years later."[3] Thus Hitchens blithely concludes: "The New Testament is itself a highly dubious source."[4] Earlier, in a chapter titled, "The Evil of the 'New' Testament," Hitchens "defers" to the journalist H. L. Mencken—an atheist and admirer of Friedrich Nietzsche—in criticizing the New Testament in colorful but vague terms: "a helter-skelter accumulation of more or less discordant documents, some of them probably of respectable origin but others palpably apocryphal."[5] The four Gospels, Hitchens snorts, are not "in any sense a historical record"[6] as the authors "cannot agree on anything of importance."[7] In so writing, he refers to the Birth of Christ, Mary, Joseph, the flight to Egypt, the Sermon on the Mount, the baptism of Jesus, Judas's betrayal, Peter's denial, the Crucifixion, and the Resurrection—apparently unaware that all of those figures and events *are* important and the Gospels do agree that Jesus was born to Mary, his foster father was Joseph, the family fled to Egypt, that Jesus gave a sermon on the Mount (as well as parables and other discourses), that Judas (not, say, Thomas)

---

[2]   Christopher Hitchens, *God Is Not Great: How Religious Poisons Everything* (New York: Twelve, 2007).

[3]   Ibid., 142.

[4]   Ibid. Hitchens's best-selling book is not well referenced; he does not specify which of Ehrman's books he is drawing upon.

[5]   Ibid, 110, quoted in H. L. Mencken, *Treatise on the Gods* (Baltimore, MD: The John Hopkins University Press, 1997), 176.

[6]   Ibid.

[7]   Ibid., 111.

betrayed him and Peter (not James) denied him, that he was arrested, questioned, tortured, crucified, buried, and rose again. As we will see later, there are a number of essential events in the Gospels that historians across the spectrums of faith and personal philosophy accept as real events, based on the criteria used in studying ancient texts.

Consider an analogy: Imagine if you interviewed players, coaches, and fans who were a part of the first Super Bowl on January 15, 1967, in which the Green Bay Packers beat the Kansas City Chiefs, 35-10. You ask them, "What time did the game start? Who scored the first touchdown? Who was the MVP? Who televised the game?" And so forth. Now imagine that Super Bowl I took place in 1776, prior to television, radio, and other modern technologies and means of archiving and communicating information. And let's say you interviewed the participants twenty, thirty, or fifty years after the game. If you received some different answers to the questions, would you immediately assume the game never happened?

Now consider this date: January 11, 49 B.C. That is one of the most famous dates in the history of ancient Rome, even of the ancient world. On that date Julius Caesar crossed the Rubicon River, committing himself and his followers to civil war. Few, if any, historians doubt that Caesar did indeed cross the river. However, if skeptics who claim that the Gospels of Matthew, Mark, Luke, and John are myths and have no basis in historical fact applied the same standards to Julius Caesar, there would be no crossing of the Rubicon; it would be dismissed as the stuff of legend and unworthy of any historical stature.

Why? Because, as historian Paul Merkley pointed out three decades ago in his article "The Gospels as Historical Testimony," there is far less historical evidence for the crossing of the Rubicon than there is for the events depicted in the Gospels:

> There are no firsthand testimonies to Caesar's having crossed the Rubicon (wherever it was). Caesar himself makes no mention in his memoirs of crossing any river. Four historians belonging to the next two or three generations do mention a Rubicon River, and claim that Caesar crossed it. They are: Velleius Paterculus (c. 19 B.C.–c. 30 A.D.); Plutarch (c. 46–120 A.D.); Suetonius (75–160); and Appian (second century.) All of these evidently depended on the one published eye-witness account, that of Asinius Pollio (76 B.C.–c. 4 A.D.), which account has disappeared without a trace. No manuscript copies for any of these secondary sources is to be found earlier than several hundred years after their composition.[8]

Merkley observed that those skeptics who either scoff at the historical reliability of the Gospels or reject them outright as "myth" do so without much, if any, regard for the nature of history in general and the contents of Matthew, Mark, Luke, and John in particular.

Again, this is something we will return to several times and in several ways. But it is important, I think, to reiterate a point made at the start of the Introduction about the message of the Apostles and first Christians. The noted New Testament scholar Craig A. Evans, author of several academic and popular books on the historical Jesus, with a focus on the Jewish background of New Testament times, sums it up well:

> The message that runs throughout the New Testament writings and the earliest Christian communities was that God had raised Jesus, to which Peter and many others (including one or two noncommitted persons such as Jesus' brothers James and perhaps Jude, and at least one opponent, Paul) bore witness. It was the reality of the

---

[8]   Paul Merkley, "The Gospels as Historical Testimony," *The Evangelical Quarterly* 58.4 (1986), 319–36.

resurrection and its impact on those who heard and responded to it in faith that propelled the new movement forward, not "mistake-free" Scripture. . . . Nonexperts perhaps need to be told that in the first ten to fifteen years of the existence of the Church, not one book of the New Testament was in existence. Nevertheless, the church grew fast and furious, without benefit of a New Testament or the Gospels (inerrant or otherwise).[9]

And that fact—the Church's fast and furious growth—is one of many significant facts Christians have long emphasized in making a case for the truth of the Resurrection.

Q. But why this fixation on the Resurrection? Why is it important whether Jesus rose from the dead—especially when it seems to be entirely a matter of faith?

How often do people rise from the dead? Doesn't it matter whether someone rose from the dead? Especially someone who taught as Jesus taught and made the sort of claims about God, salvation, and his own role in the work of God's kingdom that Jesus made?

Skeptics, of course, claim that no one can rise from the dead, or insist that no one can *prove* that someone can rise from the dead. They say it's impossible and insist—quite adamantly—that impossible things don't happen, by definition. On the other hand, even people who aren't skeptics think people don't *usually* rise from the dead. If Jesus of Nazareth did so, this is an extraordinary truth. Given the sort of things Jesus

---

[9] Craig A. Evans, *Fabricating Jesus: How Modern Scholars Distort the Gospels* (Downers Grove, IL: IVP Books, 2006), 29. Evans makes this particular point, it should be noted, in addressing Ehrman's argument that scribal errors in the Bible manuscripts "really do disprove verbal inspiration and inerrancy, so that the Bible really should be viewed as a human book and not as God's words" (p. 27).

of Nazareth said and did, if he rose from the dead, it would suggest some special power operating in his life. It would tend to corroborate the idea of God vindicating Jesus's claims and his teaching.

Fr. Gerald O'Collins, SJ, has noted how the Apostle Paul often refers to the work and power of God in raising Jesus from the dead. "We were buried therefore with him by baptism into death," Paul wrote to the Roman Christians, "so that as Christ was raised from the dead by the glory of the Father, we too might walk in newness of life" (Rom 6:4). He describes himself to the Galatians as "an apostle—not from men nor through man, but through Jesus Christ and God the Father, who raised him from the dead" (Gal 1:1). O'Collins observes that Paul "takes the Resurrection of Jesus (together with ours) as the specifically Christian way of presenting God. To be wrong about the resurrection is to 'misrepresent' God essentially, since Paul defines God as the God of resurrection" (1 Cor 15:15).[10] It is a reminder of how the distinctively Christian beliefs in God as Trinity, the Incarnation, and the Resurrection are intimately connected; if one of them is false, the others are also likely false—or cannot mean what Christians have historically claimed they meant.

In short, Christianity without a risen Christ—truly alive and with a real, glorified body—is an essentially empty, even false, belief system. "If Jesus didn't literally rise from the dead," argues philosopher David Baggett, "then at most we would have to settle for a demythologized and deflationary analysis of Christianity. The fact is, classical Christianity

---

[10] Gerald O'Collins, SJ, *Jesus Our Redeemer: A Christian Approach to Salvation* (Oxford University Press, 2007), 243. Fr. O'Collins taught theology at the Gregorian University in Rome for three decades and has written several books on the life and meaning of Jesus Christ.

would be false, and Jesus likely a philosopher at best or a madman at worst. If Jesus did bodily rise from the grave, what could be more important as a clue to the meaning of life? The resurrection matters."[11] The stakes, in other words, are high; it really is an all-or-nothing proposition.

Q. Doesn't this focus on supposed supernatural events simply feed the perception that Christianity is too heavenly minded to be of any earthly good, to borrow from Oliver Wendell Holmes?

There are, without doubt, some Christians who think that since the world appears to be going downhill—or "going to hell," as some would put it—they will simply await their heavenly reward, won for them by Christ through his Death and Resurrection. One can sympathize, at times, with such a reaction, but it is not healthy or wise, nor does it reflect a robust and authentic Christianity. On the contrary, the Resurrection does not free us from responsibilities in this world, but provides us with the spiritual strength to live as we ought as well as the spiritual insight to understand the meaning of this life and reality of the life to come.

To take up just one important example: if there is no life beyond the grave, how can most people find or obtain justice in this world? If we live this short, brutish life and then are extinguished forever, what sort of hope can be offered right now to those who are poor, invalid, starving, and suffering? And why would we be motivated to attend to their needs?

---

[11] Antony Flew and Gary Haberman, *Did the Resurrection Happen: A Conversation with Gary Habermas and Antony Flew*, ed. David J. Baggett (Downer's Grove, IL: IVP Books, 2009), 107. From the section, "Resurrection Matters: Assessing the Habermas/Flew Discussion."

This matter of justice was taken up by Pope Benedict XVI in his encyclical *Spe Salvi*, on Christian hope, who links it directly to the Resurrection and the Last Judgment:

> At the conclusion of the central section of the Church's great Credo—the part that recounts the mystery of Christ, from his eternal birth of the Father and his temporal birth of the Virgin Mary, through his Cross and Resurrection to the second coming—we find the phrase: "he will come again in glory to judge the living and the dead." From the earliest times, the prospect of the Judgment has influenced Christians in their daily living as a criterion by which to order their present life, as a summons to their conscience, and at the same time as hope in God's justice. Faith in Christ has never looked merely backwards or merely upwards, but always also forwards to the hour of justice that the Lord repeatedly proclaimed. This looking ahead has given Christianity its importance for the present moment.[12]

In other words, if Christians really do believe that Christ rose from the dead and that we can, by God's grace and power, also be raised from the dead and live in eternal glory, it should have a remarkable—even radical—effect on how they treat neighbors and strangers alike. Ironically, as Benedict pointed out, as belief in the Last Judgment has faded in modern times, people have been tempted to believe that a "world marked by so much injustice, innocent suffering, and cynicism of power cannot be the work of a good God."[13] Without God (or without a truly good God), man seeks to establish justice in ways that have, sadly, resulted in even greater injustices: "It is no accident that this idea has led to the greatest forms of cruelty and violations of justice; rather, it is grounded in the intrinsic

---

[12] Benedict XVI, *Spe Salvi* (Vatican City: Libreria Editrice Vaticana, 2007), 41. http://w2.vatican.va/content/benedict-xvi/en/encyclicals/documents/hf_ben-xvi_enc_20071130_spe-salvi.html.

[13] Ibid., 42.

falsity of the claim. A world that has to create its own justice
is a world without hope. No one and nothing can answer for
centuries of suffering. No one and nothing can guarantee that
the cynicism of power—whatever beguiling ideological mask
it adopts—will cease to dominate the world."[14]

God, in becoming man, shared in "man's God-forsaken
condition" and showed us that not only is there a God, but
that "God can create justice in a way that we cannot conceive,
yet we can begin to grasp it through faith. Yes, there is a
resurrection of the flesh. There is justice."[15] In what other way
can man's innate and powerful hunger for justice be satisfied?
"To protest against God in the name of justice is not helpful,"
stated Benedict,

> A world without God is a world without hope (*cf.* Eph 2:12). Only
> God can create justice. And faith gives us the certainty that he does
> so. The image of the Last Judgment is not primarily an image of
> terror, but an image of hope; for us it may even be the decisive
> image of hope. Is it not also a frightening image? I would say: it is an
> image that evokes responsibility, an image, therefore, of that fear of
> which Saint Hilary spoke when he said that all our fear has its place
> in love. God is justice and creates justice. This is our consolation
> and our hope. And in his justice there is also grace. This we know
> by turning our gaze to the crucified and risen Christ.[16]

This is not simply poetic language or abstract theological
lingo; it is the recognition that the Resurrection actually helps
us make sense of who we are, what we are made for, and how
we can address the sufferings and injustices so prevalent in
this world. This is why the German philosopher Josef Pieper

---

[14] Ibid.
[15] Ibid., 43.
[16] Ibid., 44.

(1904–97), in his book on the theological virtues of faith, hope, and love, stated, "In the virtue of hope more than any other, man understands and affirms that he is a creature, that he has been created by God."[17] Philosophers, he wrote, would not describe hope as a "virtue" unless they also happened to be Christian theologians. "For hope is either a theological virtue or not a virtue at all,"[18] he writes. So Pieper argues that hope—the desire for fulfillment beyond what is found in time and history, not merely the "hope" for good health or a long life—makes no sense unless there is indeed a personal and loving God. So personal and loving, in fact, that he became man, suffered, died, and rose again.

We should note that the word "hope"—much like the words "faith" and "love"—is often misused and even abused. It is easy to forget, as Pieper reminds us, "the fundamentally incomprehensible fact that hope, as a virtue, is something wholly supernatural."[19] It is why Christians say, in reciting the *Credo*: "I look for the resurrection of the dead, and the life of the world to come." Without that hope, there is no hope at all. Without a heavenly perspective, rooted in the Resurrection of Jesus Christ, we really cannot offer authentic, lasting hope to a world desperate for meaning beyond this material realm. And so it behooves us to study and understand Christ in the light of that supernatural horizon.

"One thing is clear from the beginning of Christian literature," explains Fr. Brian E. Daley, SJ, in his study of early Christian beliefs about eschatology, "hope for the future is an inseparable, integral dimension of Christian faith, and

---

[17] Josef Pieper, *Faith, Hope, Love* (San Francisco: Ignatius Press, 1997), 98.

[18] Ibid., 99.

[19] Ibid., 105.

the implied condition of possibility for responsible Christian action in the world. . . . Hope, for the Christian disciple, is the indispensable link between faith and love: the affirmation of real possibilities for the world and oneself, the awareness of a promise for the future, which gives to the person of faith the freedom to give himself or herself away, to God and to his or her neighbor."[20] That hope, springing from the Christian faith, "is clearly a hope centered on the risen Christ."[21]

Q. But isn't it enough to understand the Resurrection and the judgment to come in spiritual terms? Why the insistence on a bodily resurrection?

This will be addressed further when we examine the nature of the Resurrection in Chapter 3, but the answer is rooted— again!—in the nature of God. Christians believe that the Triune God did not create the cosmos and mankind out of necessity, but out of divine love, the eternal exchange of perfect communion and self-gift between the Father, Son, and Holy Spirit. And all that he created is good: creation is good; the material realm is good; the body is good.[22]

As Daley shows, the early Christians stood firm in their belief that there will be a bodily resurrection, befitting God's

---

[20] Brian E. Daley, SJ, *The Hope of the Early Church: A Handbook of Patristic Eschatology* (Grand Rapids, MI: Baker Academic, 2010), 217.

[21] Ibid.

[22] There persists a widespread belief, for various reasons, among many non-Christians that Christianity believes the material world is evil or bad in some moral sense. But the *Catechism* states, very directly: "Because creation comes forth from God's goodness, it shares in that goodness—'And God saw that it was good . . . very good'—for God willed creation as a gift addressed to man, an inheritance destined for and entrusted to him. On many occasions the Church has had to defend the goodness of creation, including that of the physical world" (*CCC*, 299).

direct activity—through creation and the Incarnation—in the material world. Hope in this bodily resurrection is found, for example, in the writings of Irenaeus of Lyons, who defended Christian belief from Gnostic attacks in the second century. "Hope in such a resurrection is an integral part of the Christian tradition of faith Irenaeus is concerned to protect,"[23] writes Daley. "Irenaeus insists on the fleshly reality of risen bodies: only such a hope can take seriously God's involvement with his creation,"[24] as seen in this passage from Irenaeus, written around A.D. 180:

> But vain in every respect are they who despise the entire dispensation of God, and disallow the salvation of the flesh, and treat with contempt its regeneration, maintaining that it is not capable of incorruption. But if this indeed do not attain salvation, then neither did the Lord redeem us with His blood, nor is the cup of the Eucharist the communion of His blood, nor the bread which we break the communion of His body. For blood can only come from veins and flesh, and whatsoever else makes up the substance of man, such as the Word of God was actually made. By His own blood he redeemed us, as also His apostle declares, "In whom we have redemption through His blood, even the remission of sins." And as we are His members, we are also nourished by means of the creation (and He Himself grants the creation to us, for He causes His sun to rise, and sends rain when He wills). He has acknowledged the cup (which is a part of the creation) as His own blood, from which He bedews our blood; and the bread (also a part of the creation) He has established as His own body, from which He gives increase to our bodies.[25]

Many other examples could be given, but suffice it to say for our purposes here that the early Christian testimony on the

---

[23] Brian E. Daley, SJ, *The Hope of the Early Church*, 30.
[24] Ibid.
[25] Irenaeus, *Adversus haereses,* Book 5.2.2.

bodily nature of the Resurrection and on the resurrection to come is consistent and unanimous, rooted in the belief that God's creation is good and that God "became flesh and dwelt among us" (Jn 1:14) in order to redeem men and women in their entirety: body, soul, and spirit. Belief in the Resurrection cannot be severed from belief in the Incarnation and the life and teachings of Jesus.

Q. So what sort of claims did Jesus make about himself? What sort of teaching did he propose? Why should we think he was anything more than a wise teacher?

It is, of course, difficult to summarize the claims and teaching of Jesus in an accessible and concise way. The author of John's Gospel makes this point rather poetically when he says that, in addition to what he wrote about Jesus, "there are also many other things which Jesus did; were every one of them to be written, I suppose the world itself could not contain the books that would be written" (Jn 21:25).

That said, the following are five essential points for having a solid, well-rounded understanding of who Jesus claimed to be:

1. Jesus claimed that in his ministry and person the Kingdom of God had arrived in a special way. "Repent," Jesus proclaimed, "for the kingdom of heaven is at hand" (Mt 4:17), was a message that he repeated and emphasized in many different ways. He linked it directly to his ministry—"But if it is by the Spirit of God that I cast out demons, then the kingdom of God has come upon you" (Mt 12:28)—as well as to his authority: "I will give you the keys of the kingdom of heaven, and whatever you bind on earth shall be

bound in heaven, and whatever you loose on earth shall be loosed in heaven" (Mt 16:19).

2. Jesus claimed the divine authority of the Son of Man figure mentioned in key passages of the Old Testament (*cf.* Dan 7:13). For instance, he told his disciples, "Behold, we are going up to Jerusalem, and everything that is written of the Son of man by the prophets will be accomplished," (Lk 18:31) connecting that fulfillment to his approaching arrest, Crucifixion, and Resurrection (*cf.* Lk 18:32–33).

3. He claimed he had the authority to forgive sins and to interpret correctly the Law of God given in the Old Testament. He told the paralytic, "Take heart, my son; your sins are forgiven" (Mt 9:2) before healing him, and granted the Apostles the power to forgive sins in his name: "If you forgive the sins of any, they are forgiven; if you retain the sins of any, they are retained" (Jn 20:23). Jesus explained, "Do not think that I have come to abolish the law and the prophets . . . but to fulfill them. For truly, I say to you, till heaven and earth pass away, not an iota, not a dot, will pass from the law until all is accomplished" (Mt 5:17–18). In debating the law with the Pharisees, he flatly stated, "The Son of man is lord of the sabbath" (Lk 6:5).

4. Jesus claimed to have the authority to act as the God of Israel among his people, to bring people back to God's plan for them. This is summarized in his statement about his approach to death: "'And I, when I am lifted up from the earth, will draw all men to

myself.' He said this to show by what death he was to die" (Jn 12:32–33). As Bishop Robert Barron explains:

> So when Jesus of Nazareth said, "The time is fulfilled, and the kingdom of God has come near; repent, and believe in the good news" (Mark 1:15), he was not calling attention to general, timeless spiritual truths, nor was he urging people to make a decision for God; he was telling his listeners that Yahweh was actively gathering the people of Israel and, indirectly, all people into a new salvific order, and he was insisting that his hearers conform themselves to the new state of affairs. In this gathering, he was implying, the forgiveness of sins—the overcoming of sundering and division—would be realized. In a word, the proclamation of the kingdom was tantamount to an announcement that the Gatherer of Israel had arrived and had commenced his work.[26]

5. In short, Jesus presented himself as the Son of the Father, possessing the authority of God himself. This is evident in all four Gospels, but especially in the fourth Gospel, where Jesus speaks at great length and in profound detail about his unique relationship with the Father, culminating in his claim: "I and the Father are one" (Jn 10:30; *cf.* Jn 1:18)—a statement that enraged the religious leaders, who sought to stone him because of it.

On the basis of those and other claims, Jesus taught how we should understand and relate to God and one another. Six points are noteworthy here:

1. Jesus taught love of God and love of neighbor as the supreme laws, summarizing and even deepening the

---

[26] Robert Barron, *The Priority of Christ: Toward a Postliberal Catholicism* (Grand Rapids, MI: Brazos Press, 2007), 72.

moral requirements of the Ten Commandments. The Sermon on the Mount (*cf.* Mt 5–7; Lk 6) is especially important, for it is a new law and perfect law, given on a mount—a new Sinai—by the new Moses. Jesus said: "You have heard that it was said, 'You shall love your neighbor and hate your enemy.' But I say to you, 'Love your enemies and pray for those who persecute you'" (Mt 5:43–44).

2. He established among the Jewish people a widely inclusive community of followers (disciples), led by a special group called the Twelve, with one of them, Peter, as leader. This group recalled the twelve patriarchs of Israel, which implied that Jesus regarded himself and the Twelve as renewing Israel (essentially the Jewish people) and helping it fulfill its mission to restore the unity of a divided humanity by sharing with them the truth about God and his purpose for mankind.

   During his public ministry, Jesus took his Apostles to Caesarea Philippi, north of Israel, and stood with them in front of the tall cliff that housed the many altars of pagan gods. There, Jesus told Peter, "And I tell you, you are Peter, and on this rock I will build my *Ekklesia*, and the gates of Hades shall not prevail against it" (Mt 16:18). The word *ekklesia* is from two Greek terms—*ek* and *kaleo*—meaning "to call out," referring to a called people, an assembly, formed for a unique and unifying mission.

3. Jesus saw his Death at the hands of the Jewish leadership and the Romans as the consequence of his faithfulness to God's purpose and as offering atonement

for the sins of the world. He told Nicodemus, the Pharisee who secretly visited him in the night,

> "And as Moses lifted up the serpent in the wilderness, so must the Son of man be lifted up, that whoever believes in him may have eternal life. For God so loved the world that he gave his only Son, that whoever believes in him should not perish but have eternal life. For God sent the Son into the world, not to condemn the world, but that the world might be saved through him." (Jn 3:14–17)

4. On the night before he died, Jesus established for his followers a sacrificial communal meal, based on the Jewish Passover meal, and which he identified with the imminent offering of himself in his Death on the Cross. The significance of this cannot be overstated. In his recent and exhaustive study of Jesus and the Last Supper, Dr. Brant Pitre asserts:

> When the Last Supper and Jesus' related words and deeds are situated within the triple contexts of ancient Judaism, his public life and ministry, and the rise of the early church, they strongly suggest that Jesus saw himself as the new Moses who would inaugurate the long-awaited new exodus, set in motion by a new Passover, bring back the miracle of the manna from heaven, and gather the twelve tribes of Israel into the heavenly and eschatological kingdom of God—all by means of his sacrificial death and the prophetic sign of his death that he performed at the Last Supper.[27]

5. Jesus promised to send the Spirit of God to guide his followers and to empower them to carry on his work

---

[27] Brant Pitre, *Jesus and the Last Supper* (Grand Rapids, MI: William B. Eerdmans Publishing Company, 2015), 3.

until he returned at the end of history. In the "Farewell Prayer," or "High Priestly Prayer" (Jn 14–17), the longest prayer of Jesus in the Gospels, the promise of a Paraclete, or Counselor—the Holy Spirit—is given (*cf.* Jn 14:26, 15:26). He said:

> "When the Spirit of truth comes, he will guide you into all the truth; for he will not speak on his own authority, but whatever he hears he will speak, and he will declare to you the things that are to come." (Jn 16:13)

6. He promised his Resurrection as a sign of his identity and his authority to do the things he did. As his public ministry unfolded, Jesus revealed to his disciples that he would die and rise from the grave:

> And he began to teach them that the Son of man must suffer many things, and be rejected by the elders and the chief priests and the scribes, and be killed, and after three days rise again. (Mk 8:31; *cf.* Mk 10:34; Lk 18:33)

CHAPTER 2

The Historical Reliability of the Gospels

Q. You seem to assume that we can accept the gospels as, well, "gospel truth." But doesn't most contemporary scholarship indicate, or even prove, that Matthew, Mark, Luke, and John are not historically reliable? And if they aren't historically reliable, why should anyone take them seriously when it comes to their descriptions of the Resurrection of Jesus?

Those are big, important questions, and so we will spend some time on them. After all, as you indicate, if the writings attributed to Matthew, Mark, Luke, and John really cannot be taken seriously as historical documents, shouldn't we just as well argue for the historical existence of Luke Skywalker based on the assumption that the *Star Wars* movies and stories are historically accurate? Or, to take a common example used by some atheists: believing in the existence of Jesus (or God, as the "argument" is often presented), never mind his Resurrection from the dead, is like believing in the existence of Santa Claus. We are told, as kids, that Santa Claus exists, but then we eventually learn that he does not exist—at least not as the jolly, plump man in red who is not bound by the laws of gravity or the laws of physics.[1] How is belief in the stories found in the four gospels any different?

---

[1] For the sake of argument, I'll set aside the fact that the modern

There are three basic points to be made here. First, while Santa Claus was, from the very start—apparently the late 1700s, and then Americanized by Washington Irving in his 1809 book *History of New York*—a character known and understood to be fictional but presented to some as real, Jesus of Nazareth was understood from the beginning as real, but then was presented later by some as fictional. Put another way, while some eighteenth-century Enlightenment thinkers, certain nineteenth-century liberal German Protestants, assorted twentieth-century skeptics, and cynical twenty-first-century "new atheists" claimed that Jesus was not real, the first followers of Jesus—including the authors of the Gospels and the Apostle Paul—most certainly did. And so strongly did those first-century men believe in both Jesus's existence and his teachings, almost all of them willingly died for their beliefs.[2] So far, no one has turned up evidence of anyone accepting martyrdom for belief in Santa Claus.

Secondly, and closely related, a large number of these various, modern critics (whether scholars or otherwise) carried out their investigations of the Resurrection accounts and the historical character of the early Christian belief in Jesus's Resurrection using anti-supernatural, anti-miraculist presuppositions. It is their philosophical assumptions,[3] not the historical facts or sound reasoning,

creation of "Santa Claus" was based on a real, historical man: St. Nicholas of Myra (270–343), the fourth-century Bishop of Myra, in Asia Minor.

[2] The one exception was John, author of the fourth Gospel and probable author of the Book of Revelation, who was sent into exile and died an old man.

[3] Some recent, popular critiques of such skeptical presuppositions include *The Last Superstition: A Refutation of the New Atheism* (South Bend, IN: St. Augustine's Press, 2012) by Edward Feser; *Answering Atheism: How*

that led them to their skeptical conclusions. The argument of this book is when you look at the evidence without those rationalist, anti-supernatural presuppositions, you come to very different conclusions. Again, it's imperative to note the *fact* that the earliest Christians believed and proclaimed that Jesus rose from the dead, as seen in the New Testament writings, as well as in other early, non-canonical writings. The Apostles and many others who had been close to Jesus claimed to have seen the risen Christ. Paul, initially an enemy of Christianity and of Christ, claimed to have seen the risen Christ. The argument made throughout this book is that the belief that Jesus did, in fact, rise from the dead best accounts for the *historical* evidence.

Third, having said that, there is and will continue to be a wide range of conclusions and assertions made by historians who specialize in studying the New Testament and early Christianity. There are a lot of different scholars—Christian, Jewish, agnostic, and so forth—writing specialized books on nearly every possible aspect of the Gospels and the life of Christ. However, as Bart Ehrman noted above in the Introduction, few if any scholars think or argue that Jesus did not exist. Just as significantly, the fog of skepticism that settled upon Scripture scholarship in the nineteenth and twentieth centuries has not only lifted in recent decades, it has increasingly been pierced by the clear light of a new and rigorous body of scholarship. There is a renewed recognition that the four Gospels have to be taken seriously as historical

---

to Make the Case for God with Logic and Charity (San Diego: Catholic Answers Press, 2013) by Trent Horn; God Is No Delusion: A Refutation of Richard Dawkins (San Francisco: Ignatius Press, 2011) by Thomas Crean, OP; and Atheist Delusions: The Christian Revolution and Its Fashionable Enemies (New Haven, CT: Yale University Press, 2009) by David Bentley Hart.

texts, especially mindful of the first-century Jewish context, as works meant to be not just theological in nature but also biographical and historical—not because they are accepted by Christians as canonical but because they are the earliest and best sources that exist, period. The noted New Testament scholar Craig S. Keener explains:

> We cannot know much very specific about Jesus (that would distinguish him from any other Galilean of his generation) apart from documents about him stemming from the generations immediately following him. Apart from a brief report in Josephus and mentions in two Roman historians, we are dependent especially on those most apt to preserve reports about Jesus, that is, those to whom he most mattered—his followers. We may talk about their "biases" toward him, but ultimately we have little beyond these sources to work with, and if we want to talk about the "historical Jesus," we must focus on the nature of our sources.[4]

As Keener points out, contrary to what some modern writers assume, the "bias" of the gospel writers doesn't mean their biographies of Christ are novelistic or fictional. All ancient historians had a certain "bias"; in fact, all historians have a "bias," if by that we mean coming from a certain perspective and holding specific beliefs about the subject at hand. The key is recognizing and acknowledging one's perspectives—or what New Testament scholar Michael R. Licona calls "horizons"[5]—in assessing information, analyz-

---

[4]   Craig S. Keener, *The Historical Jesus of the Gospels* (Grand Rapids, MI: William B. Eerdmans Publishing Company, 2009), 72.

[5]   "Horizons may be defined as one's 'preunderstanding.' It is how historians view things as a result of their knowledge, experience, beliefs, education, cultural conditionings, preferences, presuppositions and worldview. Horizons are like sunglasses through which a historian looks. Everything is colored by that horizon. . . . No historian is exempt." Michael R. Licona, *The Resurrection of Jesus: A New Historiographical Approach* (Downers Grove, IL: IVP Academic, 2010), 38–39.

ing texts, and reaching conclusions. And so it is no surprise that historians and other scholars end up with such a wide array of understandings of who Jesus was and what he did, but often revealing more, arguably, about themselves than about Jesus.

Q. What do you mean by that? Can you give an example?

Examples abound: many atheists or skeptics, as we've discussed, insist that Jesus didn't even exist, or that if he did, he is either lost in the mists of time or misused by Christian zealots. Rationalists of a more moderate sort tend to depict Jesus as a moral philosopher or a well-intentioned but somewhat deluded teacher. Socialists often present Jesus as a proto-Marxist and liberation leader whose struggle was ultimately political and oriented toward this world, without any real religious or spiritual focus. Other leftists paint a portrait of Jesus the community organizer, or community agitator, or both. Denizens of the New Age realm regularly equate Jesus with Buddha and speak of "Christ-consciousness." Some Christians speak of a friendly, all-inclusive Jesus who hardly warrants interest, much less worship, while others preach of a Jesus who is judging and angry, and hardly warrants charity, let alone discipleship.[6]

---

[6] The prolific Evangelical scholar Ben Witherington III, in *The Jesus Quest: The Third Search for the Jew of Nazareth* (Downers Grove, IL: InterVarsity Press, 1997), outlines some of the various approaches taken to the life and person of Jesus in the late twentieth century by Scriptural scholars. They include "Jesus the Talking Head," "Jesus the Itinerant Cynic Philosopher," "Jesus, Man of the Spirit," "Jesus the Eschatological Prophet," "Jesus the Prophet of Social Change," "Jesus the Sage," and "Jesus: Marginal Jew or Jewish Messiah?"

Some of these "Christs" are simply false and have, thankfully, been largely assigned to the ash heap of faddish history. Some are, from a Christian perspective, simply heretical—that is, knowingly contrary to the witness and teaching of the Church, Scripture, and Tradition. "Every heresy has been an effort to narrow the Church," wrote G. K. Chesterton in *St. Francis of Assisi*.[7] Likewise, these heresies can cause people to narrow and limit the person of Jesus Christ.

In the second half of the nineteenth century, "'liberal lives' of Jesus continued to flow from the German academic presses up to the turn of the century," writes Charlotte Allen in her excellent study of the search for the historical Jesus:

> Using the Gospel of Mark as their narrative skeleton, they portrayed Jesus as a man of humble origins who discovered only in adulthood that he had a divine calling, which he gradually revealed to his disciples with the instruction they keep it secret. While his miracles were mostly psychic phenomena, his teachings bore a close resemblance to the "fatherhood-of-God-brotherhood-of-men" message of the deist Jesus of the 18th century. Indeed, Jesus's messianic aims were so "spiritualized" that they amounted to little more than a sense of ethical mission.[8]

Most of what Jesus said, according to these mostly German-authored books, was either concocted by later writers and thus fictional, or was meant to be understood in a symbolic or spiritual sense and therefore free of the dogmatic and

---

[7]　G. K. Chesterton, *St. Francis of Assisi* (Garden City, NY: Image Books, 1957), 154.

[8]　Charlotte Allen, *The Human Christ: The Search for the Historical Jesus* (New York: The Free Press, 1998), 168. Allen's book is a well-researched and accessible guide to the quest to identify a "historical Jesus."

ritualistic characteristics the liberal Protestant authors found so offensive in both Judaism and Catholicism.

The strength of the temptation to create a Christ in one's own image is hard to overstate. The liberal Protestant theologian Albert Schweitzer, in the opening pages of his famous and influential 1906 book, *The Quest of the Historical Jesus*, admitted:

> For Reinhard, Hess, Paulus, and the rest of the rationalistic writers He is the admirable revealer of true virtue, which is coincident with right reason. Thus each successive epoch of theology found its own thoughts in Jesus; that was, indeed, the only way in which it could make Him live.
>
> But it was not only each epoch that found its reflection in Jesus; each individual created Him in accordance with his own character. There is no historical task which so reveals a man's true self as the writing of a Life of Jesus.[9]

Schweitzer, by the way, essentially believed that Jesus was a failed eschatological prophet. More recently, controversial scholar John Dominic Crossan—who posits that Jesus's body was most likely eaten by dogs after being removed from the Cross—admitted that the "stunning diversity" of perspectives on Jesus "is an academic embarrassment. It is impossible to avoid the suspicion that historical Jesus research is a very safe place to do theology and call it history, to do autobiography and call it biography."[10] Crossan's theory about the body of

---

[9]   Albert Schweitzer, *The Quest of the Historical Jesus: A Critical Study of Its Progress from Reimarus to Wrede*, trans. W. Montgomery, first English edition (Great Britain: A&C Black, Ltd., 1910), Chapter 1, "The Problem," www.earlychristianwritings.com/schweitzer/chapter1.html.

[10] John Dominic Crossan, *The Historical Jesus* (New York: HarperCollins, 1991), as quoted in Licona's *The Resurrection of Jesus: A New Historiographical Approach*, 47.

Christ, it should be noted, is a decidedly minority position within the stunningly diversified academic realm.

This is a notable point since orthodox Christians who hold to a traditional view of the life, Death, and Resurrection of Christ are often depicted or dismissed as simply toeing "the company line"—as if it is only the skeptic who has some sort of magical bead on objective truth, even if he denies the existence of objective truth! I noted that Ehrman, now an agnostic, was once a conservative Evangelical; I will note here that Keener, widely regarded as one of the finest New Testament scholars writing today, was once an atheist.[11] And we should not overlook the fact, to be discussed more later, that the Jewish rabbi Paul was a zealous persecutor of the early Christians prior to having an encounter with the risen Christ while on the road to Damascus (*cf.* Acts 9:1–27, 22:1–21; 1 Cor 15:8).

Q. You remarked on the first-century Jewish context. Isn't that something historians would see as quite meaningful in studying the life of Jesus, regardless of their own beliefs?

As Allen notes, foundational to those many nineteenth-century "lives of Jesus" was "a universal condemnation of the Jews. In the minds of the liberal Protestants, first-century Judaism was a stand-in for Catholicism and other forms of orthodox religion."[12] In the first half of the twentieth century, Scriptural scholarship continued to suffer, in many ways, under the sway of liberal and skeptical approaches, especially by the work of the German Lutheran theologian Rudolf Karl Bultmann (1884–1976), author of several influential books

---

[11]   Licona, *The Resurrection of Jesus*, 51.
[12]   Allen, *The Human Christ*, 169.

on Jesus, the New Testament, primitive Christianity, and mythology. While Bultmann addressed the Jewish context of Jesus's time, he focused on what he thought was unique to Jesus, to the point of downplaying the Jewish character of Jesus's words and actions.[13] Bultmann, like many other scholars of his time, asserted that the Jesus presented in the Gospel of John was a variation on the gnostic redeemer myth,[14] which was a pre-Christian understanding of God and salvation that had little, if any, direct relation to Judaism, being entirely Greek in origin.

However, the discovery of the Nag Hammadi texts and Dead Sea Scrolls in the late 1940s and early 1950s inspired a deep, even ground-breaking, interest in first-century Judaism, especially since the Scrolls revealed that many images and ideas found in the New Testament—"angels and demons, heavenly

---

[13] See Walter P. Weaver's *The Historical Jesus in the Twentieth Century: 1900–1950* (Harrisburg, PA: Trinity Press International, 1999), 103–9.

[14] A. K. Helmbold, in his article "Nag Hammedi Literature" in *The International Standard Bible Encyclopedia*, discusses the "Reitzenstein-Bultmann thesis that early Christianity freely borrowed existing Gnostic terms and beliefs." Richard August Reitzenstein (1861–1931) was a German classical philologist and scholar of Ancient Greek religion and Gnosticism whose belief that Christianity was shaped by an earlier Gnostic redeemer myth had a great influence on Bultmann, who, writes Helmbold, was "convinced that Reitzenstein had demonstrated the existence of the redeemer myth long before the 1st cent. A.D." Bultmann, in writing about the Gospel of John, explained that the basic elements of the Gnostic myth of redemption involved a heavenly being coming to earth, which was under the power of demonic forces, taking the form of man, carrying out the will of the Father, and teaching his followers how to return to their rightful home, before rising again. But following the discovery of the Nag Hammadi texts in Egypt and the Dead Sea Scrolls (near the Dead Sea, in the West Bank) in the 1940s and 1950s, that theory was rejected by many scholars, who were better able to date and trace the origins of the early Gnostic beliefs. See *The International Standard Bible Encyclopedia,* vol. 3, ed. Geoffrey W. Bromiley (Grand Rapids, MI: William B. Eerdmans Publishing Company, 1986), 475.

ascents, eschatological dramas, divine emanations, light-and-darkness metaphors, and even the title 'son of God' "[15]—were not fabricated out of whole cloth by Christians nor stolen from Hellenistic culture (as many Enlightenment-era authors claimed), but came from the Jewish culture and spirituality of the time. And more scholars began to acknowledge that the Gospel of John, far from being mythological, is far more deeply rooted in first-century Jewish thought and culture than previously thought. The main point here, of course, is that the historical foundations of Jesus's life, Death, and Resurrection, as depicted by the four Gospels, have been increasingly reasserted, more deeply mined, and studied in far more detail than before.

Fast forward, to choose a very recent example, to Brant Pitre's book *Jesus and the Last Supper*, which draws upon the same rich reservoir of ancient Jewish writings and history as did Pitre's earlier study, *Jesus, the Tribulation, and the End of the Exile*.[16] Today, observes Pitre, "it is all but universally recognized by scholars that Jesus of Nazareth was born, lived, and died a Jew. Perhaps more than any other tenet of contemporary Jesus research, the Jewish identity of Jesus has commanded a widespread acceptance, and represents a virtual consensus."[17] Pitre then gives several representative quotes from agnostic, Catholic, Protestant, and Jewish scholars, all

---

[15] Allen, *The Human Christ*, 285–86.

[16] Brant Pitre, *Jesus, the Tribulation, and the End of the Exile: Restoration Eschatology and the Origin of the Atonement* (Grand Rapids, MI: Baker Academic, 2006).

[17] Brant Pitre, *Jesus and the Last Supper* (Grand Rapids, MI: Eerdmans, 2015), 3–4. "In short," Pitre writes, "the importance of Jesus' Jewish identity and context has become one of those extremely rare occasions where virtually everyone in the scholarly realm agrees upon a basic conclusion and treats it as settled" (p. 5).

of them insisting that Jesus cannot be understood or studied properly without beginning with the fact that he was a first-century Jew from Galilee.

Q. You mentioned that the Gospels are some form of biography. But wouldn't you agree that trustworthy biographies are built on facts and eye witness accounts, not on stories told by illiterate fishermen decades after the events? Why shouldn't the Gospels, and their accounts of Jesus's life—especially miraculous elements—be viewed with suspicion?

Let me answer by first quoting Keener's observation: "Readers viewed the Gospels as biographies of some sort from the mid-second century through most of the nineteenth century."[18] That was, in other words, the nearly unanimous understanding of the Gospels for 1800 years. But many modern scholars, ranging from certain liberal European scholars such as Schweitzer to publicity-seeking groups such as The Jesus Seminar, questioned the ability of the gospels to be factual and accurate, going so far in some cases as to dismiss those texts as mostly mythological or fabricated in nature; the notion that they are "biographical" in any meaningful sense of the descriptive is essentially tossed out the door. So, for example, the Jesus Seminar—a group of 75–200 New Testament scholars that began meeting in 1985 to discuss and vote on specific texts and topics in the Gospels—concluded that only 20% of the statements attributed to Jesus in the Gospels are likely to have been uttered by him.[19]

---

[18]   Keener, *The Historical Jesus of the Gospels*, 74.
[19]   Accessed at www.theopedia.com/jesus-seminar.

A full critique of such approaches is not possible here, of course, but in general such rhetoric rests both on the assumption that the Gospels are wishful myth or calculated fiction, and that the authors of the New Testament (and their readers) were casual, clueless, or calculating about the difference between historical events and fictional stories. There is an overbearing sense of chronological snobbery at work, as if to say, "We are smarter than people who lived 2,000 years ago because we know the difference between real history and unlearned, fanciful legends."

Yet, to give just a couple of examples, the second epistle of Peter demonstrates a clear understanding of the difference between myth and verified historical events: "For we did not follow cleverly devised myths when we made known to you the power and coming of our Lord Jesus Christ, but we were eyewitnesses of his majesty" (2 Pet 1:16). Meanwhile, the opening verses of Luke's Gospel indicate that the author undertook the task of writing about real people and events:

> Inasmuch as many have undertaken to compile a narrative of the things which have been accomplished among us, just as they were delivered to us by those who from the beginning were eyewitnesses and ministers of the word, it seemed good to me also, having followed all things closely for some time past, to write an orderly account for you, most excellent Theoph'ilus, that you may know the truth concerning the things of which you have been informed. (Lk 1:1–4)

The phrase "from the beginning," argues Anglican scholar Richard Bauckham, is a specific "claim that the eyewitnesses had been present throughout the events from the appropriate commencement of the author's history onward."[20] In other

---

[20] Richard Bauckham, *Jesus and the Eyewitnesses: The Gospels as Eyewitness Testimony* (Grand Rapids, MI: William B. Eerdmans Publishing Com-

words, Luke was intent on using primary sources—people who saw and experienced firsthand what he recorded in his Gospel. The fourth Gospel concludes with an emphatic statement that echoes that understanding of how and why the Gospels were produced:

> This is the disciple who is bearing witness to these things, and who has written these things; and we know that his testimony is true.
>
> But there are also many other things which Jesus did; were every one of them to be written, I suppose that the world itself could not contain the books that would be written. (Jn 21:24–25)

This means, argues Bauckham, that "the Beloved Disciple composed the Gospel, whether or not he wielded the pen. He could have received assistance of various kinds in the process of composition or his work could have been edited by someone else, but the statement requires that he was substantially responsible for the content and for the words of the book."[21] Bauckham, of course, goes into great scholarly detail and addresses a wide range of positions in seeking to show that the Gospels were not written by men many times removed from the events described therein, but by either direct eyewitnesses or men who had spoken to direct eyewitnesses.

These three passages of Scripture do not, of course, *prove* the historicity of the New Testament. Rather, they suggest quite pointedly that the authors, far from being knuckle-dragging simpletons, set about to write works depicting real people

---

pany, 2006), 119. As the book's dust jacket states, Bauckham "argues that the four Gospels are closely based on the eyewitness testimony of those who personally knew Jesus." In doing so, Bauckham "challenges readers to end the classic division between the 'historical Jesus' and the 'Christ of faith,' proposing instead the 'Jesus of testimony' as presented by the Gospels."

[21] Ibid., 362.

and events—especially since they believed the narratives they recounted *had meaning only if they really did occur*. As such, their *historical* content should be judged not against tales of unicorns and Santa Claus, but against other first-century works of history and historical narrative.

The word "gospel" comes from the Greek word *euangelion*, meaning "good news" and refers to the message of Christian belief in the person of Jesus Christ. There has, of course, been much scholarly debate about the genre of "gospel" and how it might relate to other forms of writings found in first-century Palestine and the larger ancient world. Obviously, they do contain biographical details, and more and more scholars have argued in recent years that the Gospels are as biographical in nature as anything in the ancient Greco-Roman world.

Keener, in summarizing a substantial amount of material on ancient biographies and histories, concludes: "Clearly the Gospels are not mythography, novels, or pure drama. As works focused on a single, historical character, drawing on significant amounts of historical tradition, the Gospels are readily recognized as ancient biography."[22] And while ancient biographies differ from modern biographies in certain ways—for instance, they often did not concern themselves with following a chronological sequence, they sometimes used rhetorical devices intended for purposes of persuasion, and they usually were very open about their philosophical or theological perspectives—they "were supposed to deal in historical information rather than the fanciful creation of events."[23]

---

[22] Keener, *The Historical Jesus of the Gospels*, 84.
[23] Ibid. For more details, see Section II of *The Historical Jesus of the Gospels*, "The Character of the Gospels," 71–161.

The Catholic theologian and biblical scholar Erasmo Leiva-Merikakis, in his multi-volumed commentary on the Gospel of Matthew, sums up the nature of Gospels in this way:

> We must conclude, then, that the genre of the Gospel is not that of pure "history"; but neither is it that of myth, fairy tale, or legend. In fact, *evangelion* constitutes a genre all its own, a surprising novelty in the literature of the ancient world. Matthew does not seek to be "objective" in a scientific or legal sense. He is writing as one whose life has been drastically changed by the encounter with Jesus of Nazareth. Hence, he is proposing to his listeners an objective reality of history, but offered as kerygma, that is, as a proclamation that bears personal witness to the radical difference that reality has already made in his life.[24]

Many early Christian authors, such as Justin Martyr, referred to the Gospels as memoirs of the Apostles. Some modern scholars have used the descriptive "theological biographies,"[25] which provides a good sense of the supernatural and human elements found within them while also indicating the historical foundations involved.

Q. What are some examples of historical details in the Gospels?

There are many references, for instance, made to secular rulers and leaders—Caesar Augustus, Pontius Pilate, Herod,

---

[24] Erasmo Leiva-Merikakis, *Fire of Mercy, Heart of the Word (Vol. II): Meditations on the Gospel According to St. Matthew* (San Francisco: Ignatius Press, 2003), 44.

[25] See, for example, Craig L. Blomberg's *The Historical Reliability of the Gospels*, Second Edition (Downers Grove, IL: IVP Academic, 2007), 301–3. Blomberg notes that he uses this descriptive "in the broad sense of focusing on one central historical character as the main subject of the narrative throughout" (p. 302).

Felix, Archelaus, Agrippa, Gallio—as well as Jewish leaders—Caiaphas, Ananias—the sort of names unlikely to be
used accurately in a "myth" or even show up in that genre.
Anglican scholar Paul Barnett provides several pages worth
of intersections between biblical and non-biblical sources
regarding historical events and persons. "Christian sources
contribute, on an equal footing with non-Christian sources," he observed, "pieces of information that form part of
the fabric of known history. In matters of historical detail,
the Christian writers are as valuable to the historian as the
non-Christian."[26]

There are specifically Jewish details, including references
to and descriptions of festivals, religious traditions, farming
and fishing equipment, buildings, trades, social structures,
and religious hierarchies. As numerous books and articles
have shown in recent decades, the beliefs and ideas found in
the Gospels accurately reflect a first-century Jewish context.
One fascinating example of this is *Jesus Through Middle
Eastern Eyes*, whose author, Kenneth E. Bailey, spent forty
years living and teaching New Testament in Egypt, Leb-
anon, Jerusalem, and Cyprus. It delves into the particular
idioms, expressions, and images used in the Gospels by
clearing away certain modern, Western misunderstandings
about the specific context in which they were employed. "I
am convinced," writes Bailey, "that the Gospels are history
theologically interpreted."[27]

Various modern archaeological discoveries have validat-
ed specific details found in the Gospels. In 1961 a mosaic

---

[26] Paul Barnett, *Is the New Testament Reliable?* Revised ed. (Downers
Grove, IL: InterVarsity Press, 2003), 167.

[27] Kenneth E. Bailey, *Jesus Through Middle Eastern Eyes: Cultural Studies
in the Gospels* (Downers Grove, IL: IVP Academic, 2008), 20.

from the third century was found in Caesarea Maritima that had the name "Nazareth" in it. This is the first known ancient non-biblical reference to Nazareth. Coins with the names of the Herod family have been discovered, including the names of Herod the king, Herod the tetrarch of Galilee (who killed John the Baptist), Herod Agrippa I (who killed James Zebedee), and Herod Agrippa II (before whom Paul testified). In 1990 an ossuary was found inscribed with the Aramaic words, "Joseph son of Caiaphas," believed to be a reference to the high priest Caiaphas. In 1968 an ossuary was discovered near Jerusalem bearing the bones of a man who had been executed by crucifixion in the first century. These are the only known remains of a man crucified in Roman Palestine, and verify the descriptions given in the Gospels of Jesus's Crucifixion. And in June 1961 Italian archaeologists excavating an ancient Roman amphitheater near Caesarea-on-the-Sea (Maritima) uncovered a limestone block. On its face is an inscription (part of a larger dedication to Tiberius Caesar) that reads: "Pontius Pilate, Prefect of Judaea." Numerous other finds continue to demolish the notion that the Gospels are mythologies filled with fictional names and events.[28]

Finally, there are extra-biblical, ancient references to Jesus and early Christianity. Although the amount of non-Christian Roman writings from the first half of the first century is quite small (just a few volumes), there are a couple of significant references.

---

[28] For a popular but detailed overview of such archaeological evidence, see Robert J. Hutchinson's *Searching for Jesus: New Discoveries in the Quest for Jesus of Nazareth—And How They Confirm the Gospel Accounts* (Nashville, TN: Nelson Books, 2015), 91–115.

Writing to the Emperor Trajan around A.D. 112, Pliny the Younger (A.D. 61–113) reported on the trials of certain Christians arrested by the Romans. He noted that those who are "really Christians" would never curse Christ:

> They asserted, however, that the sum and substance of their fault or error had been that they were accustomed to meet on a fixed day before dawn and sing responsively a hymn to Christ as to a god, and to bind themselves by oath, not to some crime, but not to commit fraud, theft, or adultery, not falsify their trust, nor to refuse to return a trust when called upon to do so.[29]

The historian Tacitus (c. A.D. 56–c. 120), in his *Annals*—considered by historians to be one the finest works of ancient Roman history—mentioned how the Emperor Nero, following the fire in Rome in 64, persecuted Christians in order to draw attention away from himself. The passage is noteworthy as an unfriendly source because although Tacitus thought Nero was appalling, he also despised the foreign and, to him, superstitious religion of Christianity:

> Hence to suppress the rumor, he falsely charged with the guilt, and punished Christians, who were hated for their enormities. Christus, the founder of the name, was put to death by Pontius Pilate, procurator of Judea in the reign of Tiberius: but the pernicious superstition, repressed for a time broke out again, not only through Judea, where the mischief originated, but through the city of Rome also, where all things hideous and shameful from every part of the world find their center and become popular.[30]

Robert E. Van Voorst, author of *Jesus Outside the New Testament*, offers a detailed analysis of scholarly controversies about this passage, and then states, "Of all the Roman authors,

---

29   Pliny the Younger, *Letters*, Book 10, Letter 96.
30   Tacitus, *Annals*, 15:44.

Tacitus gives us the most precise information about Christ."[31] This includes Tacitus's understanding that "Christus"—not Paul or someone else—was the founder of the Christian movement, he notes that Christ was executed under Pilate during the reign of Tiberius and that Judea was the source of the Christian movement.

Q. But if Jesus really was divine and he really did rise from the dead, why weren't there many more books written about him during and immediately after his life?

We must keep in mind, first, that having not just one or two but four books written about a first-century Jewish man who was not rich or a king is very unusual. Few ancient works of biography and history focus on people who are not wealthy or powerful. Secondly, there is even more than the four Gospels, since we have other first-century writings by Paul and other New Testament authors that talk about Jesus in great detail.

While debate continues as to the exact dating of the Gospels, few biblical scholars believe that any of the four works were written after the end of the first century. "Liberal New Testament scholars today," writes Craig L. Blomberg, "tend to put Mark a few years one side or the other of A.D. 70, Matthew and Luke-Acts sometime in the 80s, and John in the 90s."[32] Meanwhile, many conservative scholars date the Synoptic Gospels (and Acts) in the 60s, and John in the

---

[31] Robert E. Van Voorst, *Jesus Outside the New Testament: An Introduction to the Ancient Evidence* (Grand Rapids, MI: William B. Eerdmans Publishing Company, 2000), 45.

[32] Craig L. Blomberg, *Making Sense of the New Testament: Three Crucial Questions* (Grand Rapids, MI: Baker Academic, 2004), 25.

90s. Which means, simply, that there exist four accounts of
key events in Jesus's life written within thirty to sixty years
after his Crucifixion—and this within a culture that placed
a strong emphasis on the role and place of an accurate oral
tradition. Anyone who denies that Jesus existed or who
claims that the Gospels are filled with historical errors or
fabrications will, in good conscience, have to explain why
they don't make the same assessment about the historical
works of Pliny the Younger, Suetonius, Julius Caesar, Livy,
Josephus, Tacitus, and other classical authors.

Finally, there is the sheer amount of ancient copies of the
New Testament. There are close to 5,700 full or partial Greek
New Testament manuscripts in existence. Most of these
date from between the second to sixteenth century, with the
oldest, known as Papyrus 52 (which contains John 18), dating
from around A.D. 100–150. By comparison, the average work
by a classical author—such as Tacitus (c. A.D. 56–c. 120),
Pliny the Younger (A.D. 61–113), Livy (59 B.C.–A.D. 17),
and Thucydides (460–395 B.C.)—has about twenty extant
manuscripts, the earliest copy usually several *centuries* older
than the original. For example, the earliest copy of works by
the prominent Roman historian Suetonius (A.D. 75–130) date
to A.D. 950—over 800 years after the original manuscripts
had been written.

In addition to the thousands of Greek manuscripts there
are an additional 10,000 Latin manuscripts, and thousands of
additional manuscripts in Syriac, Aramaic, and Coptic, for a
total of about 24,000 full or partial manuscripts of the New
Testament. And then there are the estimated one million
quotes from the New Testament in the writings of the Church
Fathers (A.D. 150–1300). Obviously, the more manuscripts
that are available the better scholars are able to accurately

assess what the original manuscripts contained and to correct errors that may exist in various copies.[33]

---

[33] For short but academic reviews of the various Greek manuscripts, see *The New Jerome Biblical Commentary* (Englewood Cliffs, NJ: Prentice Hall, 1990), 1104–1109, and *Dictionary of New Testament Background* (Downers Grove, IL: InterVarsity Press, 2000), 670–78.

CHAPTER 3

What Is the Resurrection?

Q. Christians call Jesus's return to life after his Death the "Resurrection" of Jesus. What does "Resurrection" mean?

It's easier to start with what it *doesn't* mean. It *doesn't* mean Jesus appeared as a ghost or the disciples saw only a vision or apparition of Jesus. Nor does it mean Jesus returned to natural life. That would be *resuscitation*, not *resurrection*. Physicians, using medicine (but not miracles), can sometimes resuscitate people who suffer "clinical death." Jesus miraculously resuscitated his friend Lazarus, who had been in the tomb for four days. The Gospel of John recounts the story in detail; it takes up forty-five verses in chapter 11, culminating in this dramatic scene:

> Then Jesus, deeply moved again, came to the tomb; it was a cave, and a stone lay upon it. Jesus said, "Take away the stone." Martha, the sister of the dead man, said to him, "Lord, by this time there will be an odor, for he has been dead four days." Jesus said to her, "Did I not tell you that if you would believe you would see the glory of God?" So they took away the stone. And Jesus lifted up his eyes and said, "Father, I thank you that you have heard me. I knew that you always hear me, but I have said this on account of the people standing by, that they may believe that you sent me." When he had said this, he cried with a loud voice, "Laz'arus, come out." The dead

man came out, his hands and feet bound with bandages, and his
face wrapped with a cloth. Jesus said to them, "Unbind him, and
let him go."

Many of the Jews therefore, who had come with Mary and had
seen what he did, believed in him. (Jn 11:38–45)[1]

Lazarus, however, died again, for while he had died and had
been restored to life, it was the same natural life he had lived
before. And Jesus was not the first prophet to bring back
someone from the dead. The prophet Elijah brought the son
of the Zarephath widow back to life after crying out to God
(*cf.* 1 Kgs 17:17–22), his successor Elisha raised the son of
the Shunammite woman from the dead (*cf.* 2 Kgs 4:32–35),
and an unnamed man was brought back to life after being
tossed into the grave of Elisha and coming into contact with
the prophet's bones (*cf.* 2 Kgs 13:20–21).[2] In all of these cases,
those who had been dead were resuscitated. Resuscitation
involves a return to natural human life, whether it occurs by
medicine or by miracle. Resuscitated people eventually die
again; they suffer the limitations of mortal existence.

Not so with resurrection, for *the* resurrection, according
to traditional Christianity, is a new and utterly unique kind
of bodily existence—not a return to ordinary human life
marked by decay, corruption, and the grave. In the Christian
view, Jesus miraculously began this new kind of existence on
Easter Sunday. He was restored to bodily existence but it was
a transformed life in which he can no longer die: "For we

---

[1]   Jesus also brought back to life the daughter of Jairus, who was the ruler
(or patron) of a synagogue (*cf.* Mt 9:18–26; Mk 5:21–43, Lk 8:40–56), and
the dead son of a widow in the city of Nain (*cf.* Lk 7:11–17).

[2]   The latter event is a text often cited in support of the ancient veneration
and care shown for the relics—most often bones, hair, or clothing—of people
recognized as saints.

know that Christ being raised from the dead will never die again; death no longer has dominion over him" (Rom 6:9). And as Paul wrote in his first epistle to the Christians in Corinth, "So is it with the resurrection of the dead. What is sown is perishable, what is raised is imperishable. It is sown in dishonor, it is raised in glory. It is sown in weakness, it is raised in power" (1 Cor 15:42–43).

This claim, notes philosopher Stephen T. Davis,

> Seems firmly embedded in the Christian tradition. For example, the Creed of Epiphanius (ca. A.D. 374) says, "The same Christ also suffered in his flesh; and he arose and ascended into heaven in that very body." The Second Council of Lyon (1274) declares, "The third day he rose from the dead by a true resurrection of the body. With the body of his resurrection and with his soul, he ascended into heaven on the fortieth day after the resurrection.[3]

Q. But don't some Christians say that they would still believe in the risen Christ even if his bones were discovered in a tomb?

Yes, they do. The late Marcus J. Borg, a prolific New Testament scholar and a key member of the Jesus Seminar, said exactly that. In a published debate with N. T. Wright, Borg rightly noted that "whatever happened on Easter, it was not resuscitation." However, he then says:

> Resuscitation intrinsically involves something happening to a corpse; resurrection need not. Resurrection does not refer to the

---

[3] Stephen T. Davis, *Risen Indeed: Making Sense of the Resurrection* (Grand Rapids, MI: William B. Eerdmans Publishing Company, 1993), 43. Davis also includes quotes from the Second Helvetic Confession (1561) and the Westminster Confession of Faith (1646). He uses those quotes as a preface to the rejection, on the part of "many theologians, biblical scholars, and clergy" of "the notion that Jesus was bodily raised" (p. 43).

resumption of protoplasmic or corpuscular existence. To be sure, resurrection could involve something happening to a corpse, namely the transformation of a corpse; but it need not. Thus, as a Christian, I am very comfortable not knowing whether or not the tomb was empty. Indeed, the discovery of Jesus's skeletal remains would not be a problem. It doesn't matter, because Easter is about resurrection, not resuscitation.[4]

There are several problems here. First, Borg appears to foist his understanding of what resurrection is—or can be—upon the writings and thought of the first Christians. Is that a logical or fair method to use? Shouldn't we be most interested in what the New Testament authors and first disciples of Jesus thought the Resurrection was or was not? Wright, of course, makes that exact point, stating the earliest Christians

cannot have meant that, though his body remained in a tomb, his spirit or soul was now safe in the hands of God, perhaps even given a place of honor. . . . Resurrection implies at the very least a coming back to something that had been forfeited, that is, bodily life. . . . What the early church insisted about Jesus was that he had been well and truly physically dead and was now well and truly physically alive. If all they had meant was that he was now exalted to a place of honor with God, the language of dying and new life the side of death would not have been appropriate.[5]

Wright also notes that if the first Christians had wanted to indicate that Jesus "was personally present with them"[6] they would have made reference to an angel or spirit. There is a distinction to be found in the New Testament between having a spiritual experience or transformation, and having seen the risen Jesus in one of his appearances.

---

[4]   Marcus J. Borg and N. T. Wright, *The Meaning of Jesus: Two Visions* (San Francisco: HarperSanFrancisco, 1999), 131.
[5]   Ibid., 116.
[6]   Ibid.

Secondly, the notion that the person of Jesus did "rise" from the dead but that the body of Jesus might remain in the tomb (or elsewhere) is an implicit but strong rejection of the Incarnation and the unity of Christ, who is one person with two distinct but perfectly united natures: human and divine. It suggests that the spiritual realm is not only superior, but that the physical realm is lesser in a problematic way—perhaps even reprehensible. Taken to its logical end, it is similar in essential respects to the various forms of gnosticism that Christians had to address and denounce so strongly in the second century and beyond.[7] A common feature of those belief systems was a radical dualism that despised the physical realm and human body, claiming that salvation was found in escaping the bonds of this material realm and the restrictive boundaries of human history.

A perfect example of this approach is found in the various writings of John Shelby Spong, who repeatedly describes as "fundamentalist" and "theistic" the traditional Christian doctrines of the Incarnation, the Virgin Birth, and the Resurrection. In short, he argues that all of those stories were added later, obscuring or even ruining, the real truth about Jesus: that he "was and is a God-presence through whom we enter the realm of the divine, a realm that transcends every religious boundary. Jesus understood that the call of every human being is not just to survive but to journey into both the fullness of one's own humanity and into the mystery of God."[8] As we saw in the Introduction, Spong rejects almost

---

[7] For a detailed examination of gnosticism and its continued influence see Carl E. Olson and Sandra Miesel's *The Da Vinci Hoax: Exposing the Errors in The Da Vinci Code* (San Francisco: Ignatius Press, 2004), especially pages 45–72.

[8] John Shelby Spong, *A New Christianity for a New World: Why*

every detail in the Gospels about the earthly life of Jesus; in this way, he is in keeping with the so-called "gnostic gospels," which have little or no interest in Jesus's earthly life, presenting Christ as a sort of enlightened being who is unfettered by the corrupting touch and influence of the physical realm. And, in a further nod to ancient gnosticism, Spong presents himself as a sort of enlightened teacher stripping away layers of authoritarian dogma and religious hysteria in order to finally—at last!—explain what really happened, beyond "the literalized and deeply inconsistent gospel stories of the resurrection. For the ability to view those resurrection stories as literal history has already exploded into an impossibility."[9] The essence of the Resurrection, Spong assures readers, "was not located in a man raised from the dead back into the life of this world. It was rather discovered when their eyes were opened to see who Jesus was and is, exalted to the right hand of God, the source of life-giving spirit, incarnate in each person as comforter and guide into all truth."[10] The story of the Resurrection, in short, "was thus not an action that occurred inside history, though when it was embraced, its effects were inside history."[11]

Spong's approach is appealing to many people for the simple reason that it is subjective and thus quite malleable to one's personal likes, interests, and perspectives; it epitomizes the "I'm spiritual, not religious" approach. Wright, in his 1992 book *Who Was Jesus?*, directly addressed the views

---

Traditional Faith Is Dying and How a New Faith is Being Born (San Francisco: HarperSanFrancisco, 2002), 138.

[9]   John Shelby Spong, *Liberating the Gospels: Reading the Bible with Jewish Eyes* (San Francisco: HarperSanFrancisco, 1996), 299.

[10]   Ibid., 305.

[11]   Ibid., 306.

of three popular writers presenting very nontraditional readings of Scripture: the Australian scholar Barbara Thiering, the British journalist and novelist A. N. Wilson,[12] and Spong. "Spong's blanket denunciation of the literal reading of Scripture," notes Wright, "leaves him wide open to the charge that, without a literal sense as the anchor, the Bible can be made to mean anything at all. When, in his concluding chapters [of *Born of a Woman: A Bishop Rethinks the Birth of Jesus*], we find the confident suggestion that Mary was pregnant with Jesus because she had been raped, and that Jesus was married to Mary Magdalene, it becomes clear that this is precisely what is happening."[13] At the end of the day, Spong's handling of the Gospels and the life of Jesus isn't much different than that found in Dan Brown's best-selling novel *The Da Vinci Code.*

Q. But isn't Spong, like many other Christians, trying to avoid a hyper-literalistic and fundamentalist misuse of Scripture?

Like me, Spong was raised in a fundamentalist home. But while Spong seems to have nothing but disdain for fundamentalism—a heavily loaded and often misused term—I find that Protestant Fundamentalism is a far more mixed (and thus complicated) matter. As Wright correctly points out

---

[12] Wilson attended an Anglican seminary as a young man, then renounced Christianity and embraced atheism for three decades. Then he announced in an April 2, 2009 *New Statesman* article that he had returned to Christianity, stating: "My departure from the Faith was like a conversion on the road to Damascus. My return was slow, hesitant, doubting. So it will always be; but I know I shall never make the same mistake again." "Why I Believe Again," http://www.newstatesman.com/religion/2009/04/conversion-experience-atheism.

[13] N. T. Wright, *Who Was Jesus?* (Grand Rapids, MI: William B. Eerdmans Publishing Company, 1992), 70.

the word "fundamentalist" has "become a way of dismissing anyone who places more weight on the Bible than one does oneself. As such, it is fairly useless."[14] Fundamentalists sometimes have a sort of "the Bible said it, I believe it" attitude that refuses to consider the complexities of how Scripture was written, compiled, edited, and produced. However, fundamentalists rightly believe, for example, that the Gospels do present truthful and historical accounts of a man, Jesus Christ, who was true God and true man, suffered, died, and rose again with a real, glorified body. In labeling such a perspective fundamentalist, Spong (and others who hold similar perspectives) is really dismissing orthodox Christianity.[15]

The deeper point here is that Spong, following in the path forged by nineteenth- and twentieth-century scholars, including Bultmann, is thoroughly modern in the sense that he believes the New Testament cannot be reconciled with a scientifically-advanced, technologically-sophisticated culture that is supposedly superior in every way from so-called "superstitious" and "primitive" notions of God and the supernatural. Exhibit A is Bultmann's famous statement, originally made in 1941:

> It is impossible to repristinate a past world picture by sheer resolve, especially a mythical world picture, now that all of our thinking is irrevocably formed by science. A blind acceptance of New Testament mythology would be simply arbitrariness; to make such acceptance a demand of faith would be to reduce faith to a work. . . . We cannot use electric lights and radios and, in the event

---

14   Ibid., 68.
15   "But if anyone who disagrees with Spong's book turns out to be fundamentalist," quips Wright, "then I suppose that all the fundamentalist churches in the world would not be able to contain the new members who would suddenly arrive on their doorsteps" (*Who Was Jesus?*, 92).

of illness, avail ourselves of modern medical and clinical means and at the same time believe in the spirit and wonder world of the New Testament.[16]

It brings to mind G. K. Chesterton's remark that "the man of the nineteenth century did not disbelieve in the Resurrection because his liberal Christianity allowed him to doubt it. He disbelieved in it because his very strict materialism did not allow him to believe it."[17] Having swallowed whole the materialist pill, Spong and like-minded thinkers are forced to basically shred and then reassemble the New Testament in Frankenstein-like fashion, creating a pathetic monster that is part pseudo-spirituality, part slavish scientism. "The modern world view is more infallible," wrote Fr. Raymond Brown decades ago, "than the first-century world view—it knows more about some things but is less perceptive in other ways. Our generation must be obedient, as were our predecessors, to what *God* has chosen to do in Jesus; and we cannot impose on the picture what we think God should have done."[18]

Q. But if a purely spiritual interpretation of the Resurrection doesn't make sense, what are the remaining options?

That's a good question because it helps bring some clarity to the big picture. We've actually already touched on three of the four essential possibilities:

---

[16] Rudolf Bultmann, *New Testament Mythology and Other Basic Writings* (Philadelphia: Fortress Press, 1989), 3–4.

[17] Gilbert K. Chesterton, *Orthodoxy* (New York: John Lane Company, 1908), 235.

[18] Raymond Brown, *The Virginal Conception and Bodily Resurrection of Jesus* (New York: Paulist Press, 1973), 72.

1. The Resurrection was a resuscitation of Jesus, who had really died and then his body was restored to its original, natural state. The Resurrection, in this view, basically "prolonged his once-interrupted life."[19]

2. The Resurrection was the raising of Jesus's spirit or "self," apart from his body, into another realm or level of existence. This is the Spiritual Resurrection Theory, and it has some variations. For instance, some who hold to it insist that Jesus does have a resurrection body but that it has no continuity with his earthly, pre-mortem body.

3. There are several reductive Resurrection theories which "in effect deny that Jesus was genuinely dead and later genuinely alive."[20] These would include psychological explanations such as visions, hallucinations, and subjective emotion experiences that inspired or created a Resurrection experience. These will be addressed in a later chapter.

4. Bodily Resurrection and transformation, in which Jesus died and then rose from the grave with a body that is on one hand the same body he had prior to death, and on the other hand is glorified and possessing unique characteristics and abilities, such as walking through closed doors, disappearing and appearing, obscuring identity. In the words of the *Catechism*:

   By means of touch and the sharing of a meal, the risen Jesus establishes direct contact with his disciples. He invites them

---

[19] Davis, *Risen Indeed*, 44.
[20] Ibid., 45.

in this way to recognize that he is not a ghost and above all to verify that the risen body in which he appears to them is the same body that had been tortured and crucified, for it still bears the traces of his Passion (*cf.* Lk 24:30, 39–40, 41–43; Jn 20:20, 27; 21:9, 13–15). Yet at the same time this authentic, real body possesses the new properties of a glorious body: not limited by space and time but able to be present how and when he wills; for Christ's humanity can no longer be confined to earth, and belongs henceforth only to the Father's divine realm (*cf.* Mt 28:9, 16–17; Lk 24:15, 36; Jn 20:14, 17, 19, 26; 21:4). . .

Christ's Resurrection was not a return to earthly life, as was the case with the raisings from the dead that he had performed before Easter: Jairus' daughter, the young man of Naim, Lazarus. These actions were miraculous events, but the persons miraculously raised returned by Jesus's power to ordinary earthly life. At some particular moment they would die again. Christ's Resurrection is essentially different. In his risen body he passes from the state of death to another life beyond time and space. At Jesus's Resurrection his body is filled with the power of the Holy Spirit: he shares the divine life in his glorious state, so that St. Paul can say that Christ is "the man of heaven" (*cf.* 1 Cor 15:35–50).[21]

Q. Some people refer to Jesus being "raised from the dead." Others speak of his "rising from the dead" or his being "risen." Do these expressions mean the same thing as "Resurrection"?

Yes. These expressions are different ways of describing what happened to Jesus after death. Being "raised from the dead," "rising from the dead," and being "risen" all point to Jesus's Resurrection, rather than a mere resuscitation or return to natural life.

---

[21] *CCC*, 645–46.

Q. Was the Resurrection also when Jesus ascended into Heaven and was exalted there by the Father?

This is a common misunderstanding, even among some Christians. It is even, as Brant Pitre points out, remarkably popular "especially among scholars who do not believe in Jesus' bodily resurrection. Nevertheless, this idea is (literally) dead wrong."[22] That is because the Ascension of Jesus into Heaven, as the creedal statements above indicate and Scripture clearly attest, took place forty days after the Resurrection; the two are entirely distinct events, even though the Ascension is made possible because of the Resurrection. The risen Jesus, in fact, told Mary Magdalene that he had not yet gone to the Father:

> Jesus said to her, "Mary." She turned and said to him in Hebrew, "Rabboni!" (which means Teacher). Jesus said to her, "Do not hold me, for I have not yet ascended to the Father; but go to my brethren and say to them, I am ascending to my Father and your Father, to my God and your God." (Jn 20:16–17)

In addition, Luke begins Acts of the Apostles by stating, "To them he presented himself alive after his passion by many proofs, appearing to them during forty days, and speaking of the kingdom of God" (Acts 1:3).

The key point here is that the Resurrection was not a spiritual event only, during which Jesus was exalted, in some form, into Heaven; rather, it was a miraculous event in which Jesus was raised from the dead with real and glorified body, becoming "the first-born from the dead" (Col 1:18; *cf.* Rev 1:5). And forty days separated that event from the Ascension, during which time Jesus, according to Paul,

---

[22] Brant Pitre, *The Case for Jesus: The Biblical and Historical Evidence for Christ* (New York: Image, 2016), 175.

"appeared to Ce'phas, then to the Twelve. Then he appeared to more than five hundred brethren at one time, most of whom are still alive, though some have fallen asleep. Then he appeared to James, then to all the apostles" (1 Cor 15:5–7).

Q. What does it mean to say that Jesus is the "first-born from the dead" (Col 1:18)?

It means that Jesus, who is the New Adam,[23] has begun and will eventually complete the work of redemption and restoration made necessary because of the Fall. The mysteries of sin and death came about because of the first Adam's failure to love and trust God, the only source of life and love. "At its heart," explains Dr. Edward Sri, "the first sin was about Adam and Eve in their pride refusing to love the God who was so good to them and rejecting God's plan of goodness for their lives."[24] This was a rupture of relationship, a severing of man from the sole means of authentic and whole existence.

The Resurrection of Jesus is the first full instance of what Christians sometimes call the New Creation, in which Jesus's disciples will later share at the end of history. This later event is also call the resurrection of the body or the resurrection of the dead. It is an idea Christians share, to some extent, with traditional Judaism and Islam. The second epistle of Peter states, "But according to his promise we wait for new heavens and a new earth in which righteousness dwells" (2 Pet 3:13). Jesus's Resurrection

---

[23] "For as by a man came death, by a man has come also the resurrection of the dead. For as in Adam all die, so also in Christ shall all be made alive. . . . Thus it is written, 'The first man Adam became a living soul'; the last Adam became a life-giving spirit" (1 Cor 15:21–22, 45).

[24] Edward Sri, *Love Unveiled: The Catholic Faith Explained* (San Francisco: Ignatius Press, 2015), 52.

and Ascension make it possible for mankind to enter into life-saving communion with God. "Therefore, if any one is in Christ," wrote Paul to the Christians in Corinth, "he is a new creation; the old has passed away, behold, the new has come" (2 Cor 5:17).

Some of Jesus's fellow Jews believed in the resurrection of the dead, which they thought would occur at the end of history. Of course, most Jews of Jesus's day did not believe *he* rose from the dead—even those who expected to be resurrected themselves one day. Those Jews who *did* believe in Jesus's Resurrection became the first Christians.

Q. Well, we've covered a fair amount of ground so far. At this point, what are the main issues surrounding the question of Jesus's Resurrection?

The main issues are: What happened to Jesus's body after his Crucifixion? What to make of early Christian claims of eyewitness encounters with the resurrected Jesus? As we've seen, we can approach those questions as matters of historical evidence; we will continue to do so in the pages to come.

We can weigh the evidence and come to some conclusions about the best answers. In the end, though, there is a third big question: What does the truth of the matter mean to *me*? How does it affect my life? That is a matter of one's personal response. People can look at a lot of evidence and listen to good, even exceptional arguments. But is that enough? We know it isn't because although there are numerous converts—including the Apostle Paul, Augustine of Hippo, Edith Stein, Chesterton, and C. S. Lewis—who have followed and presented the arguments, they did not accept and embrace Christ because of arguments alone. No, they were transformed by an encounter with the living, risen Christ. As Benedict XVI said in his Lenten message for 2011:

> The mercy of God, which cancels sin and, at the same time, allows us to experience in our lives "the mind of Christ Jesus" (Phil 2:5), is given to men and women freely. The Apostle to the Gentiles, in the Letter to the Philippians, expresses the meaning of the transformation that takes place through participation in the death and resurrection of Christ, pointing to its goal: that "I may come to know him and the power of his resurrection, and partake of his sufferings by being molded to the pattern of his death, striving towards the goal of resurrection from the dead" (Phil 3: 10–11).[25]

For believers, then, it involves a response of faith. Did God raise Jesus from the dead? If not, what of it? What does it mean for me and how do I understand Jesus? If, on the other hand, I am convinced Jesus rose from the dead and that this was an act of God, what does it mean for how I see Jesus and how I live my life? Those questions and the answers to them go beyond historical evidence, even if historical evidence can lead someone to consider them.[26]

---

[25] Benedict XVI, "Message of His Holiness Benedict XVI for Lent 2011," (Vatican City: Libreria Editrice Vaticana, November 4, 2010). http://w2.vatican.va/content/benedict-xvi/en/messages/lent/documents/hf_ben-xvi_mes_20101104_lent-2011.html.

[26] "Entering into personal relationships typically involves going beyond the evidence, as when people pledge themselves to each other in the life-long commitment of marriage.... We do not verify and justify our faith in another person simply on the grounds of historical investigation and rational argument. Something like that comes into play when believers give their allegiance to the risen Jesus, whom they experience as invisibly, yet truly, present in their lives. When they come to faith in Jesus by accepting the external testimony of the Christian community to the crucified and resurrected Jesus and the internal promptings of the Holy Spirit, they are taken beyond the evidence—specifically, the mere historical evidence. They do no base belief in the resurrection—that is to say, in the risen Christ—on historical grounds alone. Their faith is not irrational, but it is not reducible to reason." Gerald O'Collins, SJ, *Believing in the Resurrection: The Meaning and Promise of the Risen Jesus* (New York: Paulist Press, 2012), Kindle eBook.

CHAPTER 4

Accounts, Theories, and Explanations

Q. Where do we find the main accounts of Jesus's condemnation, Death, and the Resurrection appearances, and what are the main details they present to us?

The four Gospels of the New Testament contain the central and most detailed accounts of Jesus's condemnation, Death, and Resurrection. Those accounts are found in Matthew 26:57–28:20, Mark 14:53–16:20, Luke 22:47–24:53, and John 18–21.

While the accounts in the three Synoptic Gospels of the events leading up to the Resurrection are quite similar in chronology and details, the Gospel of John varies in some respects. Some of the major aspects of those accounts include:

- A conspiracy by Sanhedrin priests and the teachers of the law against Jesus.

- Jesus's triumphal entry into Jerusalem, followed by his cleansing of the Temple.

- The Last Supper prior to the Passover, held in the Upper Room, during which Jesus predicted his betrayal at the hands of Judas (who leaves the gathering) and gave instructions to his disciples.

- After the meal, Jesus prophesied that the disciples would fall away during his time of trial, and that Peter would deny him three times before the cock crowed at dawn.

- Later, in the Garden of Gethsemane, Jesus prayed in agony, asking the Father if the "cup" of his coming Passion might be taken away, but resolving that the Father's will be done. The disciples, meanwhile, went to sleep, and were eventually awakened by Jesus.

- Judas Iscariot and a crowd of soldiers and officials found Jesus and arrested him. Peter struck a servant with a sword, cutting off his ear; Jesus healed the man while the disciples fled into the night.

- Jesus was taken before the Sanhedrin, the Jewish council that handled religious and legal disputes. Before and during his interrogation by the Sanhedrin, Jesus was beaten and struck by guards. The council determined that Jesus deserved to die.

- Jesus was then sent before Pontius Pilate since the Jewish leaders did not have the authority to carry out an execution.

- Peter, in the courtyard outside the high priest's residence, was asked if he was a follower of Jesus, which Peter vehemently denied three times. Then the cock crowed and Peter recalled what Jesus had said; he then went out and wept bitterly.

- The following morning, Jesus was examined by the Roman governor, Pilate; he was found innocent, but the Jewish leaders and crowd demanded that he die.

Pilate offered them a choice between releasing Jesus or the convicted criminal Barabbas, and the people selected Jesus to be crucified.

- Judas regretted that he betrayed Jesus and tried to return the thirty pieces of silver he took in payment from the chief priests and elders. They refused the money and he threw the money in the Temple before going off to hang himself.

- Jesus was mocked, stripped, and struck by Roman soldiers, who placed a crown of thorns on his head.

- Jesus was then taken to Golgotha, or the "Place of the Skull," a hill outside the gates of Jerusalem, and crucified. A sign describing him as "King of the Jews" was placed over his head while he was mocked by the crowds watching. At noon, darkness came upon the land; at 3:00, Jesus cried out, "My God, my God, why have you forsaken me?" and then died. A spear was thrust into side and water and blood flowed out.

- The veil of the sanctuary in the Temple was torn in two and there was an earthquake; the centurion present at the foot of the Cross expressed his amazement and belief that Jesus was innocent.

- The Gospel of John recounts that Mary, the mother of Jesus, was present at his Death, along with his mother's sister, Mary of Magdala, and the disciple Jesus loved (the Apostle John).

- The events following the death of Jesus and leading up to Ascension are described in varying amounts and with somewhat different details in the Gospels.

- Matthew writes that Jesus's body was turned over to Joseph of Arimathea, a wealthy disciple, who wrapped the body in linen and "laid in his own new tomb, which he had hewn in the rock; and he rolled a great stone to the door, and departed" (Mt 27:60). Mary Magdalene and "the other Mary" sat opposite the tomb. The chief priest and Pharisees, fearing that Jesus's body might be stolen by his disciples, asked Pilate to place a guard of soldiers at the tomb; Pilate agreed, and the stone in front of the tomb was also sealed. On the morning of Sunday, the day following the Sabbath, Mary Magdalene and the other Mary went to the tomb:

> And behold, there was a great earthquake; for an angel of the Lord descended from heaven and came and rolled back the stone, and sat upon it. His appearance was like lightning, and his clothing white as snow. And for fear of him the guards trembled and became like dead men. But the angel said to the women, "Do not be afraid; for I know that you seek Jesus who was crucified. He is not here; for he has risen, as he said. Come, see the place where he lay. Then go quickly and tell his disciples that he has risen from the dead, and behold, he is going before you to Galilee; there you will see him. Behold, I have told you." So they departed quickly from the tomb with fear and great joy, and ran to tell his disciples. And behold, Jesus met them and said, "Hail!" And they came up and took hold of his feet and worshiped him. Then Jesus said to them, "Do not be afraid; go and tell my brethren to go to Galilee, and there they will see me." (Mt 28:2–10)

The guards told the chief priest what had happened; the soldiers were then given money and were instructed to tell people that the body had been stolen while they slept. That story, Matthew writes, "has been spread among the Jews to this day" (Mt 28:15). The Gospel concludes with Jesus meeting the eleven remaining disciples in Galilee: "And when they saw him they worshiped him; but some doubted" (Mt 28:17). Then Jesus gave what is often called "the Great Commission," exhorting them to go and make disciples, baptizing in the name of the Father and of the Son and of the Holy Spirit, promising them that "I am with you always, to the close of the age" (Mt 28:20).

- Mark's account is much shorter, in keeping with the more pithy, lean character of his Gospel. He adds the detail that Pilate, following the Crucifixion, personally asked the centurion if was Jesus was dead. "And when he learned from the centurion that he was dead, he granted the body to Joseph [of Arimathea]" (Mk 15:45). When the two women went the tomb on Sunday morning, they wondered who might be able to move the stone so they could anoint the body of Jesus with spices:

> And looking up, they saw that the stone was rolled back; for it was very large. And entering the tomb, they saw a young man sitting on the right side, dressed in a white robe; and they were amazed. And he said to them, "Do not be amazed; you seek Jesus of Nazareth, who was crucified. He has risen, he is not here; see the place where they laid him. But go, tell his disciples and Peter that he is going before you to Galilee; there you will see him, as he told you." And they went out and fled from the tomb; for trembling and astonishment had come upon them; and they said nothing to any one, for they were afraid. (Mk 16:4–8)

In short order, we read that Jesus appeared to Mary Magdalene, who then told the others, who did not believe her; "to two of them, as they were walking into the country" (Mk 16:12; covered in far more detail in Lk 24:13–35), whose testimony was also not accepted; and then to "the Eleven themselves as they sat at table; and he upbraided them for their unbelief and hardness of heart, because they had not believed those who saw him after he had risen" (Mk 16:14). He then commissioned them to go forth and preach, and the Gospel concludes with a short account of the Ascension.

- Luke's account is very similar to Matthew's account in many ways, but there are some differences. When the women go the tomb, they are said to have seen two men:

> And they found the stone rolled away from the tomb, but when they went in they did not find the body. While they were perplexed about this, behold, two men stood by them in dazzling apparel; and as they were frightened and bowed their faces to the ground, the men said to them, "Why do you seek the living among the dead? Remember how he told you, while he was still in Galilee, that the Son of man must be delivered into the hands of sinful men, and be crucified, and on the third day rise." And they remembered his words, and returning from the tomb they told all this to the Eleven and to all the rest. Now it was Mary Mag'dalene and Jo-an'na and Mary the mother of James and the other women with them who told this to the apostles; but these words seemed to them an idle tale, and they did not believe them. But Peter rose and ran to the tomb; stopping and looking in, he saw the linen cloths by themselves; and he went home wondering at what had happened. (Lk 24:2–12)

That is followed by the lengthy and detailed story of Cleopas and his companion traveling to Emmaus, a few miles from Jerusalem (*cf.* Lk 24:13–25). The two were approached by Jesus but "their eyes were kept from recognizing him" (Lk 24:16). They then shared the story of the Crucifixion and the testimony of the women who had seen the empty tomb. Jesus admonished them for their unbelief and lack of comprehension, and then explained "beginning with Moses and all the prophets" all the things "concerning himself" (Lk 24:27). Later, Jesus agreed to stay with them for the night:

> When he was at table with them, he took the bread and blessed, and broke it, and gave it to them. And their eyes were opened and they recognized him; and he vanished out of their sight. They said to each other, "Did not our hearts burn within us while he talked to us on the road, while he opened to us the Scriptures?" And they rose that same hour and returned to Jerusalem; and they found the Eleven gathered together and those who were with them, who said, "The Lord has risen indeed, and has appeared to Simon!" Then they told what had happened on the road, and how he was known to them in the breaking of the bread. (Lk 24:30–35)

This was followed by Jesus appearing to the startled and frightened disciples; he told them to look at his hands and feet and to touch him, "for a spirit has not flesh and bones as you see that I have" (Lk 24:39). He then ate some broiled fish in their presence (*cf.* Lk 24:39–43), before he offered explanation of what had happened, referring again to the Law of Moses, the prophets, and the psalms. Luke's Gospel ends with a brief description of the Ascension.

• The fourth Gospel, not surprisingly, provides some distinctive details. John presents the same account of Joseph of Arimathea and the burial, adding mention of Nicodemus, who brought a substantial amount of spices to use in anointing the body. On Sunday morning, after seeing the stone rolled away from the tomb, Mary Magdalene ran back to the disciples:

> So she ran, and went to Simon Peter and the other disciple, the one whom Jesus loved, and said to them, "They have taken the Lord out of the tomb, and we do not know where they have laid him." Peter then came out with the other disciple, and they went toward the tomb. They both ran, but the other disciple outran Peter and reached the tomb first; and stooping to look in, he saw the linen cloths lying there, but he did not go in. Then Simon Peter came, following him, and went into the tomb; he saw the linen cloths lying, and the napkin, which had been on his head, not lying with the linen cloths but rolled up in a place by itself. Then the other disciple, who reached the tomb first, also went in, and he saw and believed; for as yet they did not know the Scripture, that he must rise from the dead. (Jn 20:2–9)

It is then that the weeping Mary Magdalene saw two angels sitting where the body of Jesus had been. After explaining to them why she was weeping, she turned and saw Jesus standing—but, like the disciples going to Emmaus, did not immediately recognize him. When he uttered her name, she exclaimed, "Rabboni" (meaning Teacher). She then went and told the disciples, "I have seen the Lord" (Jn 20:18). Later that Sunday, Jesus appeared to the disciples (save Thomas, who was not present) who were behind locked doors; he showed them his hands and side, then breathed on them, "Receive the Holy Spirit" (Jn 20:22). Eight days later:

> His disciples were again in the house, and Thomas was with them. The doors were shut, but Jesus came and stood among them, and said, "Peace be with you." Then he said to Thomas, "Put your finger here, and see my hands; and put

out your hand, and place it in my side; do not be faithless, but believing." Thomas answered him, "My Lord and my God!" Jesus said to him, "You have believed because you have seen me. Blessed are those who have not seen and yet believe." (Jn 20:26–29)

The final chapter of John describes Jesus revealing himself again to disciples, but at the Sea of Tiberias, or Galilee. The disciples, in the midst of a failed fishing expedition, did not at first recognize Jesus, who was on the beach. After he told them to cast their net on the other side of the boat, resulting in a massive haul of fish, John told Peter, "It is the Lord!" (Jn 21:7), inspiring the impulsive Peter to jump into the water and make for shore. After eating breakfast, Jesus asked Peter three times if he, who had so recently denied his Master, loved him; Peter responded earnestly that he did, and Jesus exhorted him to tend and feed "[his] sheep." John closes his Gospel with a strong appeal to his unique stature as a direct eyewitness:

> This is the disciple who is bearing witness to these things, and who has written these things; and we know that his testimony is true.
>
> But there are also many other things which Jesus did; were every one of them to be written, I suppose that the world itself could not contain the books that would be written. (Jn 21:24–25)

Q. Are there other accounts in the New Testament of the Death and Resurrection?

The Book of Acts, written by Luke, the same author as the Gospel of Luke, also briefly discusses the Death and

Resurrection of Jesus as it introduces the story of the early Christians, most notably at the very beginning of the book (*cf.* Acts 1:1–11). The Apostle Peter, on the day of Pentecost, centered his preaching on the Death and Resurrection of his Master:

> "Men of Israel, hear these words: Jesus of Nazareth, a man attested to you by God with mighty works and wonders and signs which God did through him in your midst, as you yourselves know—this Jesus, delivered up according to the definite plan and foreknowledge of God, you crucified and killed by the hands of lawless men. But God raised him up, having loosed the pangs of death, because it was not possible for him to be held by it." (Acts 2:22–24)

Acts also recounts in three places Saul of Tarsus's encounter with the resurrected Jesus (*cf.* Acts 9:1–9, 22:6–11, 26:12–18). Saul of Tarsus, also known as Paul, became St. Paul, one of the Apostles not part of Jesus's original group of twelve. Paul is the author of over half of the New Testament, and he refers often to Jesus's Resurrection. In his own writings Paul doesn't give a detailed account of what happened but he does list some of the key witnesses who encountered the resurrected Jesus, including Peter, the Twelve, more than five hundred brethren at once, James, and Paul himself (*cf.* 1 Cor 15:3–8). The Resurrection is central to everything that Paul taught and did; he "was converted by his vision of the risen Christ. . . . It was this vision of the risen Christ that gave Paul the juridical title to his apostolate. He had been chosen as a 'witness to the resurrection,' and he joined his voice to those of the other apostles."[1]

---

[1]   Lucien Cerfaux, *Christ in the Theology of St. Paul,* trans. Geoffrey Webb and Adrian Walker (New York: Herder and Herder, 1959), 71.

The rest of the New Testament and other early Christian writings affirm Jesus's Resurrection, even though they don't go on to describe Resurrection encounters.

Q. What are the main possibilities regarding Jesus's corpse?

We've noted the theories that 1) Jesus died and rose physically but not in a glorified form; he appeared to his disciples (the Resuscitation Theory); 2) Jesus died and rose spiritually but not bodily and the disciples had a vision of Jesus as a spirit or Jesus assumed a physical form for the sake of communicating (Spiritual Resurrection Theory); and 3) Jesus died and rose in a bodily, glorified form and the disciples saw him (Resurrection).

There are also the reductive resurrection theories, which include the following:

1. Jesus didn't die on the Cross and therefore didn't rise; his disciples only thought he did (Swoon Theory);

2. Jesus died but didn't rise; his disciples hallucinated (Hallucination Theory);

3. The disciples lied about the Resurrection appearances (Conspiracy Theory);

4. They taught something different, which was later misconstrued as the Resurrection (Myth Theory).

While these four theories have enjoyed varying amounts of support from certain scholars in the past—especially in the nineteenth and early twentieth centuries—they are increasingly the property of popular speculation or assertion. And since they are so widespread in popular fiction (*The Da Vinci Code* being just one example) and in internet discussions, they deserve to be addressed. But we would do well, in light of the above overview of the biblical accounts of Jesus's Death and Resurrection, to consider this statement from Stephen T. Davis, who sums up matters very helpfully:

> Virtually all scholars who write about the resurrection of Jesus, whether they believe it happened (in some sense or other) or not, agree that (a) while early first-century Jews expected a messiah, the idea of a dying and rising messiah was new to them; (b) Jesus of Nazareth died and was buried; (c) the disciples of Jesus were consequently discouraged and dejected; (d) soon after the burial of Jesus, his tomb was claimed to be empty, and some of the disciples had experiences that they took to be encounters with the risen Jesus; (e) these experiences caused them to believe that Jesus had been raised from the dead; and (f) they started a movement that grew and thrived and that was based on the idea that Jesus had been raised from the dead. My point here is that no one who denies that Jesus was raised from the dead or who offers reductive theories of the resurrection has yet been able to account adequately for these widely accepted facts. Though many have tried, no one who rejects belief in the resurrection of Jesus has been able to tell a convincing story of what occurred in the days following his crucifixion. As noted previously, the nineteenth-century rationalistic explanations of such individuals as Reimarus and Strauss collapse on their own weight once spelled out, and skeptical twentieth-century accounts are all subject to compelling criticism. . . . The only theories that seem able to account for the accepted facts are those that affirm that Jesus was genuinely raised.[2]

With that in mind, we should spend some time addressing these various reductive theories.

---

[2] Davis, *Risen Indeed,* 180–81.

Q. Very well; let's start with the Swoon Theory. What is it and why do you think it is lacking?

It is the idea that Jesus only *appeared* to die on the Cross, when in fact he passed out or swooned. Later, he recovered in the cool of the cave tomb. Some disciples saw him emerge but they mistook him as having been resurrected. They ran to tell others. Meanwhile, Jesus succumbed to his wounds, dying unseen somewhere nearby, his body never recovered. The disciples who saw the revived Jesus misinterpreted the experience as his "Resurrection." They convinced others and thus the Christian doctrine of the Resurrection of Jesus began.

A more nefarious scenario appears in Hugh Schonfield's[3] best-selling book *The Passover Plot,* first published just over fifty years ago. In Schonfield's conspiracy-minded account, the Crucifixion and the Resurrection of Jesus were all part of an elaborate fraud, concocted by Jesus and Judas, to get Jesus proclaimed Messiah. A drugged Jesus would appear to die on the Cross. Later, he would emerge from the tomb as "risen." Unfortunately for him, the plot failed when Jesus was gravely wounded by a Roman soldier's spear (*cf.* Jn 19:34). He did reappear, only to die from his wound shortly thereafter. But not before his disciples saw him and mistakenly thought he had risen from the dead. "There was no deliberate untruth in the witness of the followers of Jesus to his resurrection," posited Schonfield. "On the evidence they had the conclusion they reached seemed inescapable. . . .Neither had there been any fraud on the part on the part of Jesus himself. He had

---

[3]   Schonfield (1901–88) was a British New Testament scholar who wrote several books offering radical theories about Jesus and the first Christians.

schemed in faith for his physical recovery, and what he expected had been frustrated by circumstances quite beyond his control."[4] That this is quite risible (Jesus schemed to deceive his followers but there was no fraud on his part?) is hardly helped by Schonfield's strange assertion—in a book full of strange assertions—that Jesus, in fact, did achieve a remarkable if accidental victory:

> The messianic programme was saved from the grave of all dead hopes to become a guiding light and inspiration to men. Wherever mankind strives to bring in the rule of justice, righteousness and peace, there the deathless presence of Jesus the Messiah is with them.... Meanwhile we have not exhausted the potentialities of the vision of Jesus.[5]

It is hardly surprising that this pseudo-scholarly theory enjoyed so much attention in the 1960s. However, the roots go back to the Enlightenment, when a German polemicist, theologian, and *enfant terrible*, Karl Friedrich Bahrdt (1741–92), outlined the same basic theory, replete with a secret Order of Essenes, elaborate conspiracies, and a Jesus who argues against miracles and wishes to overthrow the superstitious and tyrannical rule of the religious leaders. In short, Jesus is presented as an eighteenth-century German rationalist. Schweitzer describes how Bahrdt explained away all of Jesus's miracles through natural means. For instance, the feeding of the five thousand was carried out using bread the Order of Essenes had hidden in a cave, which was handed to Jesus as he stood in front of the cave's entrance. And:

---

[4]   Hugh Schonfield, *The Passover Plot: A New Interpretation of the Life and Death of Jesus* (New York: Bantam Books, 1969), 173. First published 1965.

[5]   Ibid., 174.

The walking on the sea is to be explained by supposing that Jesus walked towards the disciples over the surface of a great floating raft; while they, not being able to see the raft, must needs suppose a miracle. When Peter tried to walk on the water he failed miserably. The miracles of healing are to be attributed to the art of Luke. He also called the attention of Jesus to remarkable cases of apparent death, which He then took in hand, and restored the apparently dead to their sorrowing friends. In such cases, however, the Lord never failed expressly to inform the disciples that the persons were not really dead. They, however, did not permit this assurance to deprive them of their faith in the miracle which they felt they had themselves witnessed.[6]

The inescapable impression is that most of the followers of Jesus, including the authors of the four Gospels, were either dupes or dolts. However, the more serious problem for Schonfield and other swoon advocates is that the theory is implausible for several reasons.

Q. Why is it implausible that Jesus swooned on the Cross and then later appeared again?

There are several major problems, which together are really impossible to overcome.

First, it is highly unlikely that Jesus could have survived crucifixion, drugged or otherwise. The procedure was gruesome and lethal; that's its point. In 1986, three medical doctors co-authored an essay, "On the Physical Death of Jesus Christ," for the *The Journal of the American Medical Association* (*JAMA*), in which they detailed the excruciating trauma and torture that Jesus received at the hands of the Roman soldiers. The abstract for the article states:

---

6   Schweitzer, *The Quest of the Historical Jesus*, 41.

> Jesus of Nazareth underwent Jewish and Roman trials, was flogged, and was sentenced to death by crucifixion. The scourging produced deep stripelike lacerations and appreciable blood loss, and it probably set the stage for hypovolemic shock as evidenced by the fact that Jesus was too weakened to carry the crossbar (patibulum) to Golgotha. At the site of crucifixion his wrists were nailed to the patibulum, and after the patibulum was lifted onto the upright post, (stipes) his feet were nailed to the stipes. The major pathophysiologic effect of crucifixion was an interference with normal respirations. Accordingly, death resulted primarily from hypovolemic shock and exhaustion asphyxia. Jesus's death was ensured by the thrust of a soldier's spear into his side. Modern medical interpretation of the historical evidence indicates that Jesus was dead when taken down from the cross.[7]

The Romans were very efficient at torturing and killing people; they wouldn't have been careless to permit a controversial figure such as Jesus to survive. After all, Jesus was condemned as an enemy of the state, a false claimant to royalty and a political revolutionary. That's how Roman authority saw him. Allowing such a prisoner to escape was itself a capital offense under Roman law, so the Roman soldiers who executed Jesus had every reason to ensure his death (as indicated by Pilate asking the centurion if Jesus was really dead).[8] Likewise, the Jewish authorities who opposed Jesus would have verified that he was dead.

What's more, according to what purports to be eyewitness testimony recorded in John 19:34–35, a Roman lance pierced the crucified Jesus's side. With the torture of the brutal

---

[7]   William D. Edwards, MD, Wesley J. Gabel, MDiv, and Floyd E. Hosmer, MS, AMI, "On the Physical Death of Jesus Christ," (*The Journal of the American Medical Association,* 255 86): 1455–63.

[8]   "And Pilate wondered if he were already dead; and summoning the centurion, he asked him whether he was already dead" (Mk 15:44).

beating Jesus received and the crucifixion itself, and then the piercing of Jesus's side by a Roman spear, it seems utterly impossible that he could have swooned only to recover later.[9]

Yet even assuming, for the sake of argument, Jesus *did* somehow survive the crucifixion, a half-dead Jesus couldn't have convinced anyone of his triumphant Resurrection. If the disciples and others encountered him, they would hardly have seen him as the glorious, risen Lord; his appearing "would not have evoked their worship of his Lord. The conviction of the earliest disciples was that Jesus rose gloriously and triumphantly from the grave, not as one who had managed to barely escape death."[10]

What's more, it seems unlikely Jesus would have disappeared altogether from history without a trace. If some of the disciples saw a wounded Jesus who died shortly after, surely someone would have discovered his remains and would have used them to undercut and destroy Christian claims of Resurrection. Not only do apparent death theories make light of the basic intelligence of Jesus's followers, it does the same to the many enemies of Jesus.

According to Matthew 27:62–66, the Jewish authorities had the Romans post guards at the tomb. (Although some critics challenge the claim of guards at the tomb, we shall see

---

[9] "Since no one was intended to survive crucifixion," write the authors of the 1986 *JAMA* article, "the body was not released to the family until the soldiers were sure that the victim was dead. By custom, one of the Roman guards would pierce the body with a sword or lance. Traditionally, this had been considered a spear wound to the heart through the right side of the chest—a fatal wound probably taught to most Roman soldiers. The Shroud of Turin documents this form of injury. Moreover, the standard infantry spear, which was 5 to 6 ft (1.5 to 1.8 m) long, could easily have reached the chest of a man crucified on the customary low cross" (p. 1460).

[10] William Lane Craig, *Reasonable Faith: Christian Truth and Apologetics* (Wheaton, IL: Crossway Books, 1994), 279.

the arguments for their position are weak.) If a weakened Jesus recovered in the tomb, how could he have emerged with the guards there? How would he have unwrapped himself from the many linens which made up his death shroud (*cf.* Jn 19:40)? It is very unlikely the guards would have fallen asleep, as opponents of Christianity tried to assert (*cf.* Mt 28:11–15). And even if the guards did fall asleep, that still doesn't explain how a severely wounded Jesus could convince the disciples he had been resurrected. Consider that not only had he been beaten, scourged, and crucified, he likely had gone a substantial amount of time without rest or any form of basic sustenance.

As many Christian apologists have noted, a most devastating blow to the Swoon Theory comes from a surprising source: the nineteenth-century liberal German theologian David Strauss. In his book *A New Life of Jesus*, Strauss concludes:

> It is impossible that a being who had stolen half-dead out of the sepulchre, who crept about weak and ill, wanting medical treatment, who required bandaging, strengthening and indulgence, and who still, at last, yielded to his sufferings, could have given to the disciples the impression that he was a Conqueror over death and the grave, the Prince of Life, an impression which lay at the bottom of their future ministry. Such a resuscitation could only have weakened the impression which he had made upon them in life and in death, at the most could only have given it an elegiac voice, but could by no possibility have changed their sorrow into enthusiasm, have elevated their reverence into worship.[11]

Also, as William Lane Craig notes, the Swoon Theory is biographically implausible. "The theory says that Jesus

---

[11] David Strauss, *A New Life of Jesus*, vol. 1 (London: Williams and Norgate, 1879), 412.

tricked the disciples into believing in his resurrection. But this is a tawdry caricature of all that we know of the real Jesus, whose life and teaching belie such an interpretation of his character."[12] While historians differ about the extent to which early Christian and other accounts are historically sound, there is near complete agreement among historians that Jesus died on the Cross. That makes the Swoon Theory historically implausible as an explanation for what happened to Jesus's corpse and the Resurrection appearances.

---

[12] Craig, *Reasonable Faith*, 279.

Chapter 5

Hallucinations and Guilty Disciples?

Q. Let's say that Jesus was indeed crucified. What about the idea that Jesus's disciples hallucinated the resurrected Jesus?

According to this explanation, often called the Hallucination Theory, the disciples were so desperate to believe in the vindication of Jesus they hallucinated a Resurrection encounter. Proponents of this idea sometimes refer to "visions" of Jesus but they really mean hallucinations. The "visions" of the Hallucination Theory are subjective experiences that don't correspond to anything real. They're imaginary projections rather than objective experiences.

The Resurrection of Jesus, in this view, has nothing to do with Jesus's body, or even with Jesus's spirit, but only with what happened to the *disciples* after their encounter. They were able to cope with their teacher's death and to find a reason to continue to spread his teachings. But the Jesus they encountered was a figment of their imaginations. One irony is that while this theory has been used, of course, to attack the Christian belief in the Resurrection, it is essentially what liberal writers and theologians such as Spong, Borg, and Crossan suggest or openly posit as a *positive* outcome of Jesus's Death! In both instances, however, the evidence and logic are flawed or lacking altogether.

Strauss adhered to the Hallucination Theory, and it was quite popular in the 1800s. "About 100 years ago," explained Gary R. Habermas in a 2001 article, "the hallucination hypothesis was the most popular critical position until it passed out of scholarly favor."[1] Based on his survey "of more than 1,000 publications on the subject of Jesus' Resurrection published between 1975 and [2001],"[2] Habermas concluded that the theory has experienced a resurgence in interest and some support. Recent scholars who hold to some form of the theory include controversial German theologian Gerd Lüdemann, British biblical scholar Michael Goulder, and Jack A. Kent, the author of *The Psychological Origins of the Resurrection Myth.*

According to some critics, notably Goulder (who prefers "conversion vision" over "hallucination"), the idea of Jesus's Resurrection started with the experience of Peter, one of Jesus's main disciples, and spread to other disciples in "copy-cat" fashion. Peter was, so the argument goes, guilt-ridden for having abandoned Jesus to his fate at the hands of the Jewish and Roman authorities. After Jesus's Death, Peter had a "conversion vision" of Jesus triumphant Resurrection, which others subsequently experienced as well. Paul, too, originally an enemy of Jesus's followers, had psychological, guilt-related "issues" ultimately "resolved" by a "vision" of a triumphant Jesus. "So there is no resurrection of Jesus," states Goulder, "Psychological explanations are available for the early, appearance traditions; and known intra-ecclesial controversies about the nature of the resurrection explain

---

[1]   Gary R. Habermas, "Explaining Away Jesus' Resurrection: Hallucination," *Christian Research Journal* 23, no. 4 (2001). Accessed at http://www.equip.org/article/explaining-away-jesus-resurrection-hallucination/.

[2]   Ibid.

the Gospels additions."[3] Of Lüdemann, a Christian turned atheist, Licona notes, "Like Goulder, he appeals to the social sciences with the expectation that 'modern psychological studies' will assist us in understanding 'the rise of Easter faith.' Peter was a victim of 'self-deception.'"[4]

Lüdemann's approach, says Habermas, is similar to nine-teenth-century attempts such as those put forth by Strauss.

> [Lüdemann] holds that this explanation can be applied to all of the chief participants in the earliest church: the disciples, Paul, the 500, and James, the brother of Jesus. Lüdemann asserts that Paul's use of the term *ophthe* in 1 Corinthians 15:3ff clearly means that he was speaking of actual sight, of "his own active sensual perception. . . ," as well as that of the other apostles. So Paul "must have expected the Corinthians to understand the term historically." Lüdemann concludes that hallucinatory visions are required, along with "auditory features" that produced a "stimulus," "enthusiasm," "religious intoxication," and "ecstasy" for Peter. This spread to the other disciples by "an incomparable chain reaction." Paul, the other apostles, 500 persons, and James all similarly experienced these subjective visions. The appearances were collective, amounting to a "mass ecstasy."[5]

The logical conclusion of all this is that Christianity is the re-sult of not only mass hallucinations, but "is based on multiple mental illnesses and that its earlier converts (including those who claimed to be eyewitnesses of the resurrection) preached, quite literally, a message of madness."[6] Such a theory, I must

---

3   Quoted by Licona in *The Resurrection of Jesus: A New Historiographical Approach*, 482. Licona devotes many pages to Goulder's theory (479–95).

4   Ibid., 496–97.

5   Habermas, "Explaining Away Jesus' Resurrection: Hallucination."

6   Douglas Groothuis, *Christian Apologetics: A Comprehensive Case for Biblical Faith* (Downers Grove, IL: IVP Academic, 2011), 557.

say, requires a leap of faith that might well be described as religious—or, better, irrational.

Q. That seems a bit harsh. If the Resurrection encounters were merely subjective experiences of Jesus, don't they still amount to *real* experiences? After all, the disciples *really* had them.

While subjective experiences *are themselves real* they are not experiences *of the real*. That is, what they purport to be about isn't real—that's why they are called *hallucinations*. If the disciples experienced the risen Christ in this sense only, then Jesus's body remained in the tomb and Jesus is dead, plain and simple. Claims of the Resurrection understood in the traditional sense are false, whatever else we might say about "resurrection" in some other sense.

Q. Then what are the arguments against the Hallucination Theory?

One glaring problem with the theory is that the disciples didn't expect a resurrection of Jesus. Indeed, they initially didn't believe claims of Jesus's Resurrection (*cf.* Lk 24:11, 24; Jn 20:25). That's hardly the mindset of people ready to hallucinate an encounter with a dead man—a man many of them witnessed brutally beaten and executed on the Cross a few days before! Furthermore, nothing in Judaism as the disciples understood it inclined them to expect the Messiah would die and then rise from the dead.[7] In the first-century,

---

[7]   The expectations of first-century Jews is covered in great detail in N. T. Wright's *The Resurrection of the Son of God* (Minneapolis, Fortress Press, 2003), 32–206.

concludes N. T. Wright, there "are no traditions about a Messiah being raised to life: most Jews of this period hoped for resurrection, many Jews of this period hoped for a Messiah, but nobody put those two hopes together until the early Christians did so."[8]

The shameful execution of Jesus at the hands of Israel's enemies, the Romans, as well as his rejection by Israel's religious establishment, appear, at first glance, to be a massive *disproof* of Jesus's messianic claims. Deuteronomy 21:22–23 says that execution by hanging on a tree was a sign of God's curse, a notion the Jews also applied to crucifixion. Why then should his disciples suddenly think Jesus vindicated and triumphant as Messiah, when to all appearances he had been utterly abandoned by God and discredited? Why didn't the disciples give up their hope in Jesus? Or why didn't they embrace one of Jesus's close relatives as an alternative candidate—James, perhaps, who eventually became a leader in the early Church? It wasn't uncommon for a defeated leader's relatives or close associates to take up his mantle of leadership. Why didn't that happen with Jesus? Given the more likely options, hallucinating visions of a triumphant Jesus seems the last thing the disciples would have done, under the circumstances.

If the disciples encountered a resurrected Jesus, it would make sense for them to rethink their discouragement and to see Jesus as Messiah. They would then see him as vindicated by God raising him from the dead. They would rethink their understanding of what Jesus said and did. All those things make sense *if* the disciples saw the risen Jesus. But moving from discouragement and fear to hallucinating a victorious

---

[8] Ibid., 205.

Jesus, rather than transferring their hopes elsewhere or abandoning them altogether, makes no sense.

Besides, group hallucinations are, at best, incredibly rare, and group hallucinations in which all those present have essentially the same experience or hallucination are even more dubious.[9] Is it really logical to think that when the remaining eleven Apostles saw Jesus—not once but several times—that they were each experiencing the same vision? "It would be an understatement," Licona dryly notes, "to claim that such a proposal has only a meager possibility of reflecting what actually occurred. Embracing it would require an extraordinary amount of faith."[10] In addition, as Douglas Groothuis rightly argues, "The hallucination theory fails given the nature of hallucinations, but it also fails to explain the empty tomb."[11] The empty tomb, in fact, would be the sort of cold water that would bring most hallucinating people back to reality.

Q. What about the idea that Peter and Paul hallucinated visions of Jesus out of guilt?

The argument from Peter's guilt also falters. Even if Peter felt responsible for Jesus's Death, it's hard to understand how he would continue to believe in Jesus as a messiah figure or if he did, how it would lead to a vision of the triumphant Jesus. Peter might have felt responsible for betraying his friend but it seems unlikely he would have continued to see Jesus in the same light. His vicious execution would have discredited

---

[9] See *The Resurrection of Jesus: A New Historiographical Approach*, 484–85.

[10] Ibid., 485–86.

[11] Groothuis, *Christian Apologetics*, 557.

Jesus in Peter's eyes as much as anyone else's, however sorry he felt for his role in the events that discredited Jesus.

Similarly, even if Paul felt sorrow for his mistreatment of his fellow Jews who had become Christians, it seems implausible to posit this as the basis of a hallucination vindicating Jesus in Paul's mind. It's one thing to experience remorse for having a hand in the death of someone you regard as peddling a false messiah; it's another thing for one's guilt to lead you to embrace the false messiah as true and to hallucinate a vision of him.

Arguments from Peter's and Paul's supposed psychological states are highly speculative. This is especially true when it comes to Paul. We have no indication that prior to his encounter with the risen Jesus Paul felt guilt for persecuting Christians. Psychological explanations are *possible*, but simply because an explanation is possible doesn't mean it is *probable* or likely. We need evidence to judge a possible explanation as probable one. We lack such evidence in the cases of Peter and Paul. Nothing Paul tells us about himself allows us to account for his encounter with the resurrected Jesus as a hallucination due to guilt or other psychological factors.

Q. Are there other objections to the Hallucination Theory?

As suggested already, the range and diversity of Resurrection appearances also argue against the idea of hallucination. According to Paul, Jesus appeared to many people at different times: to Cephas (Peter), to all of the Twelve, to over five hundred disciples at once (some of whom, Paul says are still alive), to James (apparently, this refers to a so-called "Lord's brother," Jesus's relative), then all those designated "apostles," and lastly to Paul himself (*cf.* 1 Cor 15:3–8).

Scholars think the list Paul cites was a sort of an "official" list of witnesses regarded as most authoritative and reliable. Paul says he "received" the list and passed it on to the Corinthians (*cf.* 1 Cor 15:3). The "list" is probably a kind of early Christian creedal statement to which Paul has added his own testimony at the end (*cf.* 1 Cor 15:8). While mass hallucination might be invoked as an explanation for some appearances to people on the list, it's implausible as an explanation for all of them.

The list Paul cites is not exhaustive. Some of the Resurrection appearances mentioned in the Gospels are not included, such as those featuring the testimony of the women witnesses—apparently, the first people to encounter the risen Jesus. (Jewish authorities, as noted before, did not generally regard women as reliable witnesses, so the initial list may have excluded them to minimize credibility problems for Christian evangelists, even though the various Christian communities knew the women's stories.) Paul's list also leaves out the appearance to the two disciples on the road to Emmaus.

Adding together all the accounts, we see an even wider range of circumstances and variety of persons who recall or who were described as having encounters with Jesus after his death—*far too wide* a range for hallucination to be a plausible explanation.

Q. According to the Gospels, Jesus predicted his Resurrection. Why shouldn't we see these predictions as providing the basis for later hallucinations of his Resurrection?

The Gospels report that Jesus made cryptic statements about his Death and Resurrection, yet the same sources tell us his disciples didn't understand what he meant. This is more consistent with what the sources tell us about the disciples' initial general disbelief when they heard of the Resurrection than with the idea they anticipated encountering a risen Jesus. We see in the Gospels that while Jesus told the disciples that he was going to be killed and would rise again, the disciples either pushed back against it (*cf.* Mt 16:21–23) or they pushed it to the side and out of their memory (*cf.* Lk 24:6–8).

Of course as Jews, the disciples probably believed in the resurrection of the dead, as did Jesus and the Pharisees (though not the Sadducees), but the resurrection of the dead was supposed to be at the end of the world.[12] Even if Jesus's cryptic predictions did provide the disciples grounds for thinking Jesus would triumph despite his public defeat and humiliation—and we have no evidence they did—the disciples would likely have situated that triumph at the end of the world, when *all* the dead would be raised. Only if the disciples had actually encountered the risen Jesus would they have had grounds for altering their Jewish views and acknowledging at least one resurrection before the end of the world—that of Jesus.

We can imagine someone claiming to have had a vision of Jesus reigning victorious in Heaven—as Stephen did while he was being stoned to death (*cf.* Acts 7:55–56). But the earliest Christians didn't say they had seen only a vision of Jesus; they claimed that Jesus *actually rose from the dead*. That implies much more than an apparition of Jesus in the afterlife. For those Jews who affirmed the resurrection of the dead, as we have said, resurrection wasn't understood as continued existence as a spirit in the afterlife; resurrection involved a *bodily* transformation. Such a metamorphosis is what the early Christians claimed Jesus had undergone and

---

[12]   See Wright, *The Resurrection of the Son of God*, 129–206.

what they purported to have seen the results of. Besides, psychoanalyzing "persons who are not only absent but who also lived in an ancient foreign culture involves a great deal of speculation and is a very difficult and chance practice."[13] They involve many conjectures and require ignoring many pieces of evidence to the contrary.

The simple form of the Hallucination Theory fails on another count: it doesn't explain what happened to the body of Jesus or why, when Christians began preaching the Resurrection of Jesus, someone didn't undercut their message simply by producing the body or pointing to the tomb. In order to be plausible, the Hallucination Theory has to draw on other ideas—such as the Swoon Theory and the Myth Theory. We have already discussed the problems with the Swoon Theory; we will discuss the Myth Theory later.

Q. Maybe the disciples hallucinated and then simply went to the wrong tomb (Wrong Tomb Theory). Or perhaps they went to the wrong tomb, found no body, and hallucinated the Resurrection encounters. What about those explanations?

We don't really have any historical basis for thinking the disciples went to the wrong tomb. Some proponents of the Wrong Tomb Theory try to bolster their case by a *selective* use of the Gospel material. When some of Jesus's women followers, so the argument goes, unwittingly appeared at the wrong tomb on Easter Sunday morning, the young man (elsewhere depicted as an angel) who stood at the entrance told them, "He [Jesus] is not here" (Mt 28:6). Then pointing

---

[13] Craig, *The Resurrection of Jesus*, 505. Section 5.4 in this work responds to Lüdemann's "methodical skepticism."

to the appropriate tomb nearby he said, "See the place where they laid him" (Mk 16:6). In their fear and confusion, the women mistook the man to mean Jesus rose from the dead. The other disciples, coming to the same empty but erroneous tomb, likewise jumped to the wrong conclusion. Hallucinations to that effect followed.

The Wrong Tomb Theory rests on the highly improbable assumption that based on a misunderstanding of the man at the tomb, the disciples would think Jesus rose from the dead and then go on to hallucinate. It also requires us to believe the Gospel accounts correctly relate the words "He [Jesus] is not here" and "See the place where they laid him," but got wrong what was intended by them. The women were apparently (and mysteriously) reliable enough to recount those words but they weren't reliable about anything else. It also requires us arbitrarily to delete the words "He has been raised" from the man's remarks, as well as his directive to tell Peter and the other disciples about the Resurrection.

Also, the tomb is identified in all four Gospels as belonging to Joseph of Arimathea, a member of the Sanhedrin and a wealthy disciple of Jesus, thus giving a specific location known to those familiar with the places and people involved. There is no other option mentioned, and it is hard to believe that Joseph, presented as such a well-known man, was a Christian invention.[14]

The Wrong Tomb Theory also assumes the disciples would conclude that an empty tomb meant a living Jesus. Yet that is extremely unlikely since, as we have said, Jews who believed in the resurrection of the dead thought it would happen at the end of the world. There would be no reason for the disciples

---

[14] Groothuis, *Christian Apologetics*, 543.

to think a missing body meant Jesus would be resurrected before then, even if they did still believe him to be the Messiah or thought he was somehow triumphant—as unlikely as it would have been, given his Crucifixion. Furthermore, as the Gospels make clear, the empty tomb itself first suggested someone had moved the body, not that Jesus had been raised from the dead (*cf.* Jn 20:13).

Q. What about the claim that dogs ate Jesus's corpse or that it was thrown into a common grave?

There is no historical evidence such a thing happened to Jesus's body but some radical critics, such as Crossan, nevertheless claim it did, appealing to common scenarios at the time of disposing of the bodies of executed criminals. Of course, if the disciples knew Jesus's corpse had been disposed of in either of these ways, we would have to account for the emergence of the burial and empty tomb tradition. That's hard to do. All four Gospel accounts explicitly refer to Jesus's burial and to the empty tomb (*cf.* Mt 28:5–7; Mk 16:5–8; Lk 24:2–7; Jn 20:1–9). Paul refers explicitly to Jesus's burial (*cf.* 1 Cor 15:4) and implicitly—as we shall see—to the empty tomb when he recounts an early list of resurrection appearances.

Critics appeal to what they claim *usually* happened to the corpses of crucified people over what the earliest accounts say happened to Jesus *in particular*. Critics unreasonably minimize or ignore the unusual circumstances surrounding his execution. We will return to this issue when we discuss the Myth Theory.

Chapter 6

Contradictions and Conspiracies

Q. Let's return to the Gospel accounts of Jesus's burial and the events of Easter morning. How can we rely on those accounts when they do greatly differ from one another?

It is true that many critics assert that the accounts by Matthew, Mark, Luke, and John differ substantially from one another and, in some ways, cannot be reconciled. For some critics, it seems, the only thing that matters is finding differences, however nuanced or speculative, in order to cast suspicion on them. Robert Funk, the founder (and "guiding light") of the Jesus Seminar refers often to "anomalies"[1] among the accounts of the Resurrection, saying that several such accounts are viewed by scholars "as legendary expansion without historical warrant....Attempts to reconcile the reports with each other have not been successful."[2]

John Shelby Spong also calls every detail into question, insisting "we must face first the fact that the biblical witness to the events it describes as taking place at the dawn of

---

[1]   Robert Funk, *Honest To Jesus: Jesus for a New Millennium* (HarperSan-Francisco, 1996), 266.

[2]   Ibid., 267. Note that Funk does not say "some scholars" or otherwise qualify his description, apparently dismissive of the many scholars who would not agree with his sweeping judgment.

Easter day is significantly confused, contradictory, and, in some instances, mutually exclusive."[3] And, as usual, Spong fixates on the physical, literal nature of what the Gospels describe, dismissing as "fanciful"[4] the descriptions of angels and the resurrected body of a man crucified thirty-six hours earlier. "The Church," he writes, "has sought over the years to soft-pedal these contradictions, suggesting rather lamely that no five witnesses describe the same event in the same way. That is, of course, true; but when those descriptions are mutually exclusive, then our hold on any truth begins to be questioned."[5] Gary Wills asserts the same in his breezy book *What Jesus Meant*. After claiming "the empty tomb of itself means little or nothing,"[6] he states: "The apparitions in the gospels are multiple and confusing (if not contradictory)— the fruit of different communities' memory of their different founders and emissaries giving witness to what they saw."[7] One wonders, however, what such critics might say if all of the accounts neatly aligned with one another. Even apparent discrepancies, notes Davis, "testify in a left-handed way to the accuracy of the essential story: if the resurrection of Jesus were a story invented by the later Christian church, or by certain members of it, no discrepancies would have been allowed."[8]

The Muslim author Reza Aslan, in his bestselling *Zealot: The Life and Times of Jesus of Nazareth*, sums up many of the common liberal points: the Resurrection accounts were

---

[3]   Spong, *Liberating the Gospels*, 279.
[4]   Ibid.
[5]   Ibid., 280.
[6]   Gary Willis, *What Jesus Meant* (New York: Penguin, 2006), 124.
[7]   Ibid., 25.
[8]   Davis, *Risen Indeed*, 181.

not written until the 90s (at the earliest), they are part of the elaborate "theological reflections"[9] rendered by the early Christians after the destruction of the Temple by the Romans in A.D. 70, and were the result of the followers of Christ trying to make Gospel lemonade out of the lemons of the Cross:

> Precisely because the resurrection claim was so preposterous and unique, an entirely new edifice needed to be constructed to replace the one that had crumbled in the shadow of the cross. The resurrection stories in the gospels were created to do just that: to put flesh and bones upon an already accepted creed.[10]

And, "Again, these stories [about the resurrection] are not meant to be accounts of historical events; they are carefully crafted rebuttals to an argument that is taking place offscreen."[11] Of course, if they were so carefully constructed after decades of consideration, why are they said to also be confusing and contradictory?[12] You start to sense that any stick works to beat down the argument that the accounts in the four Gospels are reliable and can be taken seriously as historical narratives.

---

[9]   Reza Aslan, *Zealot: The Life and Times of Jesus of Nazareth* (New York: Random House, 2013), 173.

[10]   Ibid., 176.

[11]   Ibid., 177.

[12]   Along these same lines, Stephen T. Davis, in a chapter on the empty tomb, says he doubts the empty tomb is "an apologetic legend," as some critics assert. "The empty-tomb tradition," he argues, "just does not have the characteristics we would expect it to have if it were an inverted apologetic device, designed to convince readers that Jesus really rose. For one thing, the empty tomb does not play an apologetic role in the New Testament. . . . Far from being presented as an irrefutable argument for the resurrection, the empty tomb is rather depicted as an enigma, a puzzling fact that no one at first is able to account for" (*Risen Indeed*, 72–73). This brings to mind the creative approach taken in the 2016 film *Risen*, in which the Resurrection is depicted as a sort of historical mystery, viewed mostly from the perspective of a Roman tribune ordered by Pontius Pilate to find the missing body of Jesus.

In fact, the accounts don't greatly differ on key points and the differences of detail aren't so great that we must regard the accounts as historically unreliable. In fact, all four Gospel accounts, despite their differences in other respects, agree completely on the facts of Jesus's burial and the empty tomb. There aren't, for example, some accounts with Jesus still in the tomb and others with him out, or some accounts saying he was buried and others denying it. There are three essential facts presented in all four texts:

1. All of the Gospel accounts agree that Jesus was dead and was buried in a tomb near Jerusalem supplied by Joseph of Arimathea (*cf.* Mt 27:59–61; Mk 15:46–47; Lk 23:53; Jn 19:40–42).

2. All describe the tomb as empty on Easter morning (*cf.* Mt 28:6; Mk 16:6; Lk 24:3, 6; Jn 20:2, 6).

3. And all indicate this was because Jesus rose from the dead (*cf.* Mt 28:7; Mk 16:6–7; Lk 24:6; Jn 20:9, 11–18).

"There seem," Davis rightly notes, "no resurrection texts that question any of these items."[13] Such agreement on foundational points, despite differences of detail, tends to support the burial and empty tomb tradition's historical reliability, not undercut it. It suggests the witnesses had their own accounts and did not tailor them to make them all dovetail. Later we will examine in more detail some of the differences among the Resurrection accounts. For now it is sufficient to say they agree on the central issues of Jesus's burial, the empty tomb, and the claim that Jesus rose from the dead.

---

[13]   Davis, *Risen Indeed*, 181.

Q. If the tomb of Jesus was empty, why didn't the early Christians venerate it? The fact they didn't venerate the tomb implies they didn't think anything miraculous or special had happened there.

We have no evidence the earliest Christians *didn't* venerate the empty tomb. Certainly, later Christians recalled a tradition of veneration that became the basis for the site of the Church of the Holy Sepulcher, which most Christian traditions (Catholic, Orthodox, and Protestant) regard as the burial and Resurrection site of Jesus. The New Testament does not record Christian veneration of the tomb but we shouldn't expect it to do so. The emphasis of the New Testament is not on the empty tomb *as such* but on Jesus's *not being* there anymore. For the earliest Christians, the more important thing was that Jesus was no longer there—not that he once had been.

Q. Christian writers claim the Jewish and Roman authorities could have debunked Christianity by producing Jesus's corpse. But isn't it possible the body was too corrupt by the time Jesus's followers proclaimed the Resurrection?

The historical evidence supports the idea the disciples preached the Resurrection relatively quickly after Jesus's death—within a month and a half or so.[14] Even if Jesus's body was at that point partly decayed it wouldn't necessarily be unrecognizable. The authorities producing Jesus's corpse would have still made it hard for the disciples to preach

---

[14] On the historicity of Luke's description of events at Pentecost, see Craig S. Keener, *Acts: An Exegetical Commentary, Introduction and 1:1–2:47* (Grand Rapids, MI: Baker Academic, 2012), 90–220, 780–990.

Jesus as resurrected—and they certainly would have been motivated to produce the body of Jesus. That we have no evidence that the authorities produced the corpse suggests they had no corpse to produce because the tomb was empty and Jesus was alive. "Early Christian proclamation of the resurrection of Jesus in Jerusalem," writes Davis, "would have been psychologically and apologetically impossible without safe evidence of an empty tomb."[15]

Q. Why overlook the simplest explanation? The alleged witnesses of the risen Jesus lied. The Resurrection was a deception and a conspiracy. The disciples stole Jesus's body and then claimed they had seen him raised from the dead. This idea circulated in the early days of Christianity (*cf.* Mt 28:13–15)—so why shouldn't it be given serious consideration?

The Conspiracy Theory—which has ancient roots[16] and has also enjoyed plenty of space and attention in popular literature over the years—is highly improbable for a number of reasons. Here are three of the most significant reasons it doesn't hold up to scrutiny.

First, the teaching of Jesus and the Apostles called for truthfulness; it is based on a philosophy and dynamism of inherent integrity. If the disciples made the whole thing up, it would mean they were hypocrites and supreme liars about

---

[15] Davis, *Risen Indeed*, 79.

[16] William Lane Craig provides some historical background in *The Son Rises: The Historical Evidence for the Resurrection of Jesus* (Eugene, OR: Wipf and Stock Publishers, 2000), 23–36. Craig notes that the "theory of conspiracy by the disciples surfaced again in the seventeenth and eighteenth centuries, being supported this time by deists.... After the eighteenth century, the conspiracy theory was laid permanently to rest and never again gained the consensus of scholarship" (p. 25–26).

the most fundamental thing in their lives: their faith in Jesus Christ. That's not impossible, but it's highly unlikely. How could those who boldly emphasized the importance of truth, in the face of fierce opposition, somehow base the heart of their belief on what they would have *known* was false? It goes against everything we know about human nature, both for individuals and groups of people.

Second, people don't usually give their lives for what they *know* to be a lie, which is what the disciples would have done if they fabricated the Resurrection story. What would they have thought to gain by such a deception? They would have needed "a credible motive for such a ruse."[17] Was it power? Or money? All of the evidence says otherwise, quite dramatically so. The Jewish authorities had condemned Jesus. The Roman authorities brutally executed him. Would the leaders of the disciples have believed these same authorities would take kindly to Jesus's followers announcing a resurrected Jesus? Why should they have anticipated anything other than what they in fact received—persecution? And is it reasonable to believe that all of the alleged conspirators remained faithful to their lie until the end? That they would maintain it even in the face of death? Blaise Pascal (1623–62) would have none of it, writing in his *Pensées*:

> The hypothesis that the Apostles were knaves is quite absurd. Follow it out to the end, and imagine these twelve men meeting after Jesus's death and conspiring to say that he has risen from the dead. This means attacking all the powers that be. The human heart is singularly susceptible to fickleness, to change, to promises, to bribery. One of them had only to deny his story under these inducements,

---

[17] Groothuis, *Christian Apologetics*, 558.

or still more because of possible imprisonment, tortures and death, and they would all have been lost. Follow that out.[18]

In addition to *motive*, the Conspiracy Theory also has to account for *means*—for how the disciples were able to steal the body of Jesus, given the presence of guards at Jesus's tomb. It also has to account for why Paul, an enemy of Jesus's followers, would come to believe he had seen the risen Jesus. If the conspiracy includes Paul, we have to explain how Paul could have suffered so much for what he knew to be a lie.[19]

Q. Some critical scholars claim there were no guards at Jesus's tomb. The author of the Gospel of Matthew, they claim, made up the idea of guards at the tomb in order to counter claims that the disciples stole the body.

It is unlikely the guards at the tomb were fabricated since we have good grounds for thinking that the Jewish authorities would have wanted to ensure that Jesus's disciples wouldn't steal the body and claim to have witnessed the Resurrection.

---

[18]   Quoted by Peter Kreeft, *Christianity for Modern Pagans: Pascal's Pensées Edited, Outlined, and Explained* (San Francisco, Ignatius Press, 1993), 265, in Blaise Pascal, *Pensées*, trans. A. J. Krailsheimer. (London: Penguin Classics, 1966), 801. Kreeft adds: "The 'conspiracy theory'—that they conspired to deceive the world—is absurd; for people conspired to lie only to gain some advantage. What advantage did Christ's apostles gain? Excommunication, persecution, hatred, torture, imprisonment, crucifixion—hardly a list of perks! The amazing historical fact that not one of them ever confessed to the conspiracy, even under torture—neither did any of their successors—is very powerful evidence" (p. 266).

[19]   Groothuis makes the interesting comparison to the story of convicted Watergate felon and Christian convert Charles Colson, who wrote in his book *Loving God* (Grand Rapids, MI: Zondervan, 1983): "With the most powerful office in the world at stake, a small band of hand-picked loyalists, no more than ten of us, could not hold a conspiracy together for more than two weeks" (p. 559).

The Romans, as well, had a stake in safeguarding the tomb, given the political tensions in Jerusalem at the time and the fact of Jesus's execution for sedition. Of course, if you dismiss Jesus's predictions of the Resurrection as unhistorical, then there's little reason to think the authorities would have expected the disciples to attempt to steal Jesus's body. But we have no reasonable grounds for rejecting the idea that Jesus spoke cryptically about "rising from the dead."

Besides, if early Christian apologists *had* fabricated the story of the Roman guards, why didn't they just fabricate an appearance to Jesus's enemies, including the guards? Why didn't they concoct a story about Jesus appearing triumphantly to the high priest and the Jewish leaders who had him executed, rather than to pagan Romans, whose testimony would be dismissed by the Jews? Because the Romans and the Jewish leaders would deny the story? But wouldn't they do the same thing to the story of Roman guards posted at the tomb? If we rule out making up a Resurrection appearance to Jesus's enemies on the grounds his enemies would deny it, we should rule out making up a Roman guard posted at the tomb story on the same grounds.

Chapter 7

Mythology or Gospel Truth?

Q. Alright. But perhaps the disciples and other early followers gradually created the story of the risen Jesus. After all, don't stories have a way of growing and developing over time?

According to the Myth Theory, the Resurrection of Jesus is a myth or legend that gradually emerged over the years following Jesus's Death. The basic form of this theory posits that the idea of Resurrection developed over time, as stories circulated and teaching about Jesus became separated from the original source of his followers. Originally, Christians affirmed only some form of Jesus's survival, which they held to be vouchsafed by some kind of vision. The myth of the Resurrection came to replace this belief.

A more sophisticated version of the theory alleges an inability of the Hebrew mind to conceive of immortality apart from corporeal existence. This supposedly forced the early Christians to describe their belief in Jesus's victory over death and glorification in physical terms as resurrection. As *Jewish* Christians they supposedly lacked other categories to describe it. The Resurrection, then, would be a myth intended to express a spiritual truth about Jesus—his spiritual victory and presence with God.

Another variation, recycled by Aslan, is that Paul put aside any concerns about the historical Jesus and essentially created a new and radical idea of Jesus that was not only "extreme," it was "an altogether new doctrine that would have been utterly unrecognizable to the person upon whom he claims it is based."[1] Aslan writes:

> For it was Paul who solved the disciples' dilemma of reconciling Jesus's shameful death on the cross with the messianic expectations of the Jews, by simply discarding those expectations and transforming Jesus into a completely new creature, one that seems almost wholly of his own making: Christ.... Paul's Christ is not even human, though he has taken on the likeness of one (Philippians 2:7). He is a cosmic being who existed before time.[2]

Aslan—much like John Shelby Spong and Deepak Chopra—claims that this Pauline-fabricated Christ "has since become the standard doctrine of the church."[3] A slightly more nuanced and scholarly approach is taken by noted New Testament scholar Geza Vermes, a former priest who reverted to Judaism, who argues that Paul "adopted a completely new stance in his attitude to Jesus which distinguishes him not only from the more 'historical' Mark, Matthew, and Luke, but even from John. In ignoring the man from Nazareth and his activities in Galilee and Jerusalem, Paul had no need to incorporate into his synthesis traditional elements of the portrayal of Jesus."[4]

We can see how the Myth Theory can develop the argument of the Hallucination Theory. What began as a hallucination of Jesus, whose body remained in its grave or came to naught,

---

[1]   Aslan, *Zealot*, 188.
[2]   Ibid., 189.
[3]   Ibid.
[4]   Geza Vermes, *The Changing Faces of Jesus* (New York: Viking Compass, 2001), 83. Vermes also insists that "Paul makes no attempt whatever to anchor Christ in history" (p. 85).

gradually became, in this view, a claim to his bodily Resurrection. The first believers would have been unconcerned about Jesus's corpse, even while they claimed to have had a vision of him triumphant. Only later, after the belief in the triumphant Jesus came untethered from the original, apostolic "vision," did Christians understand it as a claim about bodily transformation and an empty tomb.

In short, a vision of the dead Jesus triumphant in Heaven was slowly but surely transformed into a dogma about his bodily Resurrection, complete with empty tomb and physical encounters with his disciples.

Q. Isn't there some truth to the arguments that Paul created Christianity? Isn't he really the myth maker when it comes to the Resurrection?

It's a good and important question since, as we've seen, Paul is often presented by certain modern critics as having taken the early, original form of Christianity and turning it into something different—even radically different. And so Paul ends up playing a central role in many of the most popular forms of the Myth Theory.

Not surprisingly, the idea that Paul created Christianity—or created what we now call Christianity—has its roots in the mid-eighteenth century and the influential Tübingen School of historical-criticism. Although David Strauss is better known today, it was the work of the Hegelian theologian Ferdinand Christian Baur (1792–1860) that began driving a wedge between Jesus and Paul. Baur—the founder of the Tübingen School of theology—used Hegel's theory of dialectic to argue that early Christianity was marked by two opposing theses, represented by "Pauline Christianity" and

"Petrine Christianity," and that a synthesis of the two was established in the second century.

In the Preface to his 1845 book, *Paul: His Life and Works*, Baur wrote:

> I advanced the assertion which I have since maintained and furnished with additional evidence, that the harmonious relation which is commonly assumed to have existed between the Apostle Paul and the Jewish Christians with the older Apostles at their head, is unhistorical, and that the conflict of the two parties whom we have to recognize upon this field entered more deeply into the life of the early Church than has been hitherto supposed.[5]

Baur's assertion soon became a chasm as more theologians (mostly German and Protestant) followed his lead. The work of two men is worth mentioning: philosopher Friedrich Nietzsche (1844–1900) and Lutheran theologian Georg Friedrich Eduard William Wrede (1859–1906). Although Nietzsche, in *The Antichrist* (1895), described Jesus as an "idiot,"[6] he reserved special hatred for "the Christianity of Paul,"[7] which he argued was radically different from the teachings of Jesus. He wrote:

---

[5] F. C. Baur, *Paul: The Apostle of Jesus Christ: His Life and Works, His Epistles and Teachings*, trans. Dr. Eduard Zeller (London: Williams and Norgate, 1876), v.

[6] This description is found in section 29 of Nietzsche's *The Antichrist* (*Der Antichrist*, 1895), and may be a reference to Fyodor Dostoyevsky's 1869 novel *The Idiot*. H. L. Mencken, in his translation of *The Antichrist* (New York: Alfred A. Knopf, 1920) left out the phrase "the word idiot" ("*das wort Idiot*"). But later English translations by Josef Hofmiller, Walter Kaufmann, and R. J. Hollingdale contain the phrase. Nietzsche viewed Jesus as a hypersensitive mystic who could not deal with material reality, "a being at home in a world which is no longer in contact with any kind of reality" (*The Antichrist*, section 29).

[7] Friedrich Wilhelm Nietzsche, *The Antichrist*, trans. H. L. Mencken (New York: Alfred A. Knopf, 1920), 80.

[Paul] represents the genius for hatred, the vision of hatred, the relentless logic of hatred. *What*, indeed, has not this dysangelist sacrificed to hatred! Above all, the Saviour: he nailed him to *his own* cross. The life, the example, the teaching, the death of Christ, the meaning and the law of the whole gospels—nothing was left of all this after that counterfeiter in hatred had reduced it to his uses. Surely *not* reality; surely *not* historical truth![8]

Nietzsche—in true Enlightenment-era fashion—claimed that Christianity, as fashioned by Paul, is simply a combination of ancient mystery religions: "the subterranean cults of all varieties."[9] Paul, in other words, was a master synthesizer of wildly divergent beliefs, the better to gain him a wide following.

Wrede, an ardent practitioner of historical criticism, wrote in his 1901 book *The Messianic Secret* that Jesus never claimed to be the Messiah. The Gospel of Mark, Wrede believed, made Jesus out to be a secret Messiah who was simply a teacher and miracle worker. In his later book, *Paul*, Wrede wrote there was "an enormous gulf between this man and the Pauline Son of God"[10] and that Paul's belief in "a celestial being"[11] and "a divine christ"[12] prior to his belief in Jesus resulted in Paul becoming "the second founder of Christianity."[13] He further argued that Paul, although a Jew, constructed a theology that was mostly Hellenistic in character. And, "If we are to

---

[8]   Ibid., 119. Nietzsche also asserted that "Paul simply shifted the center of gravity" of the life of Jesus "to the lie of the 'risen' Jesus" as he "had no use for the life of the Saviour" (p. 120).

[9]   Ibid., 171.

[10]   William Wrede, *Paul*, trans. Edward Lummis (London: Philip Green, 1907), 147.

[11]   Ibid., 151.

[12]   Ibid.

[13]   Ibid., 179.

designate the character of this conception we cannot avoid the word 'myth.' "[14]

A more recent example, on the popular level, can be found in A. N. Wilson's *Paul: The Mind of the Apostle*, which portrays Paul as a complex and enigmatic mythologizer. "The genius of Paul and the collective genius of the 'early church,'" Wilson states, "which wrote the twenty-seven surviving books we call the New Testament, was to mythologize Jesus."[15] Wilson took pains to insist he was not reviving an "old History of Religions School" or claiming that Paul "crudely invented a new religion, but that he was able to draw out the mythological implications of an old religion, and the death of a particular practitioner of that religion, and to construct therefrom a myth with reverberations much wider than the confines of Palestinian Judaism."[16] For Paul, historical fact and detail are of little interest: "The historicity of Jesus became unimportant from the moment Paul had his apocalypse."[17] A more scholarly work that comes to the same basic conclusions is *Paul: the Founder of Christianity*[18] by Gerd Lüdemann, the German theologian-turned-atheist who subscribes to the Hallucination Theory, as noted earlier.

Most of those who claim Paul created Christianity based on a mythical Christ figure with little, if any, basis in historical reality point to the small number of references in his

---

[14] Ibid.

[15] A. N. Wilson, *Paul: The Mind of the Apostle* (New York: W. W. Norton & Company, 1997), 72.

[16] Ibid., 72.

[17] Ibid., 73.

[18] Gerd Lüdemann, *Paul: the Founder of Christianity* (Amherst, NY: Prometheus Books, 2002).

writings to the teachings and life of Jesus. While Paul often mentions the Death and Resurrection of Jesus—an obviously central theme for him—there is relatively little said about Jesus's family, birth, baptism, miracles, discourses, and parables. Paul does state in several places that he is passing on information or instruction he had received from "the Lord" (1 Cor 7:10–11, 9:14, 11:23–25, 14:37; 2 Cor 12:8–9; 1 Thes 4:15–17), but he does not use direct quotes from Jesus. Critics argue he was simply using claims of personal revelations as a basis for his supposed apostolic authority. In addition, they ask why Paul doesn't quote Jesus in places where it would be to his benefit to do so. For instance, when Paul states, "I know and am persuaded in the Lord Jesus that nothing is unclean in itself; but it is unclean for any one who thinks it unclean" (Rom 14:14), why does he not refer to Jesus's teaching about food and defilement (*cf.* Mk 7:17–23)?

Q. Yes, why doesn't Paul talk more about Jesus's teaching and details about Jesus's life?

The first thing to note is that the letters of Paul are largely occasional in nature; that is, they were written to address ongoing issues and questions in churches—in Rome, for example—that were already established. They were meant to be primarily works of exhortation, not argumentation. None of them, after all, were addressed to non-believers; they were not evangelistic in nature, but aimed at exhorting, encouraging, correcting, and pastoring. Because of this, many scholars believe that Paul did not need to quote from Jesus's teaching, writes British theologian David Wenham, "because he and his readers have been taught it and know it well. In his letters his task is to discuss what is disputed and unclear, not to repeat what is already very familiar."[19]

While this argument from silence is unconvincing to many critics, it intersects very well with the second point, made by N. T. Wright, which is that Jesus and Paul had quite different roles in the "eschatological drama"[20] of salvation history. This argument rests on the priority and the validity of the Gospels, asserting that if Jesus really was the Messiah, proclaimed and established the Kingdom of God, died and rose from the dead, and ascended into Heaven, then he was completely unique. Therefore his teachings and life would have been the first things passed on by oral teaching and preaching, liturgy, and example.[21] Paul understood himself to be a "servant

---

[19] David Wenham, *Paul: Follower of Jesus or Founder of Christianity?* (Grand Rapids, MI: William B. Eerdmans Publishing Company, 1995), 5. Wenham's book is an in-depth argument for Paul being "better described as 'follower of Jesus' than as 'founder of Christianity'" (p. 33). Also see his book *Paul and Jesus: The True Story* (Grand Rapids, MI: William B. Eerdmans Publishing Company, 2002).

[20] N. T. Wright, *What Saint Paul Really Said: Was Paul of Tarsus the Real Founder of Christianity?* (Grand Rapids, MI: William B. Eerdmans Publishing Company, 1997), 179.

[21] *Dei Verbum*, the Second Vatican Council's Dogmatic Constitution on Divine Revelation, states: "In His gracious goodness, God has seen to it that what He had revealed for the salvation of all nations would abide perpetually in its full integrity and be handed on to all generations. Therefore Christ the Lord in whom the full revelation of the supreme God is brought to completion (see Cor. 1:20, 3:13, 4:6), commissioned the Apostles to preach to all men that Gospel which is the source of all saving truth and moral teaching (*cf.* Matt. 28:19–20, and Mark 16:15; Council of Trent, session IV, Decree on Scriptural Canons: Denzinger 783 [1501]), and to impart to them heavenly gifts. This Gospel had been promised in former times through the prophets, and Christ Himself had fulfilled it and promulgated it with His lips. This commission was faithfully fulfilled by the Apostles who, by their oral preaching, by example, and by observances handed on what they had received from the lips of Christ, from living with Him, and from what He did, or what they had learned through the prompting of the Holy Spirit. The commission was fulfilled, too, by those Apostles and apostolic men

of Jesus Christ, called to be an apostle, set apart for the gospel of God" (Rom 1:1); as such, Wright argues, he didn't simply "repeat Jesus' unique, one-off announcement of the kingdom to his fellow Jews. What we are looking for is not a parallel between two abstract messages. It is the appropriate continuity between two people living, and conscious of living, at different points in the eschatological timetable."[22]

Jesus believed that he had been sent by God to "bring Israel's history to its climax"[23] and Paul believed that Jesus had succeeded in this heavenly, covenantal mission. Paul was not interested in establishing a new religion or an ethical system or a syncretistic mixture of mystery religions. He was, Wright stresses, "deliberately and consciously implementing the achievement of Jesus."[24] Or, in Paul's own words:

> According to the commission of God given to me, like a skilled master builder I laid a foundation, and another man is building upon it. Let each man take care how he builds upon it. For no other foundation can any one lay than that which is laid, which is Jesus Christ. (1 Cor 3:10–11)

And part of this work—this participation in what Jesus had achieved by his Death and Resurrection—was to apply and live out the reality of this salvation in many different cultural contexts, including Palestine, Greece, Asia Minor, and Rome.

At the heart of Paul's thought and theological work, Wright explains, is the Resurrection of Christ:

---

who under the inspiration of the same Holy Spirit committed the message of salvation to writing (*cf.* Council of Trent, loc. cit.; First Vatican Council, session III, Dogmatic Constitution on the Catholic Faith, Chap. 2, "On revelation": Denzinger 1787 [3005])" (par. 7).

22 Wright, *What Saint Paul Really Said*, 181.

23 Ibid.

24 Ibid.

Everything thus hinges on Jesus's resurrection.... As far as Paul was concerned, the most important eschatological event, through which the living God had unveiled (or, if you like, "apocalypsed") his plan to save the whole cosmos, had occurred when Jesus rose from the dead. He wasn't just living in the last days. He was living in the first days—of a whole new world order. As with the cross, the resurrection permeates Paul's thinking and writing; and it isn't by any means just the future resurrection, to which of course Paul looks forward. It is the resurrection of Jesus, to which he looks back.[25]

Having said that, there are, in fact, many allusions in Paul's writings to specific, historical details from the life of Jesus. These include the following:

- Jesus was "descended from David according to the flesh" (Rom 1:3) and was also a descendant of Abraham (*cf.* Gal 3:16);

- Jesus was born and raised as a Jew (*cf.* Gal 4:4);

- The names of some of Jesus's disciples, including Cephas (*cf.* 1 Cor 9:5);

- The words and actions of Jesus at the Last Supper (*cf.* 1 Cor 11:23–25);

- The betrayal of Jesus (*cf.* 1 Cor 11:23);

- Jesus was executed by being crucified (*cf.* Phil 2:8, 3:18; 1 Cor 1:17–18; Gal 5:11; 6:12), with the assistance of certain Judeans (*cf.* 1 Thes 2:1–15);

- Jesus rose from the dead (*cf.* Rom 1:4, 4:24–25, 8:11; 1 Cor 6:14, 15:4–8; 2 Cor 4:14; Gal 1:1; 1 Thes 4:14);

---

[25]   Ibid., 50.

- After the Resurrection, Jesus "appeared to Cephas, then to the twelve" (1 Cor 15:5);

- He also appeared, post-Resurrection, to "more than five hundred brethren at one time, most of whom are still alive, though some have fallen asleep. Then he appeared to James, then to all the apostles" (1 Cor 15:6–7).

All of this indicates that Paul understood Jesus as a real, historical person, not as a mythic savior figure with little or no connection to earthly life. For first-century Jews and Greeks alike, it was taken for granted that it was only possible for a community or group to imitate the character and behavior of someone who was real and whose life was known. This is part of the reason the Gospels were written: to preserve and present the words and actions of Jesus, so that, in the words of Paul, readers would "be conformed to the image of his Son" (Rom 8:29; *cf.* 1 Cor 11:1).

Q. But even if Paul did mention details about Jesus's earthly life, wouldn't he have several years, even decades, to reformulate and even remake the meaning of Jesus's life and Death?

Some who hold to the Myth Theory give the impression that it is reasonable to think that over the course of many decades people would begin to accept a mythologized version of "the Christ," with only a tenuous relationship to the historical Jesus. The big problem, however, is that the time frame doesn't square with the theory. Martin Hengel, the renowned German scholar of New Testament and early Judaism, argues that "all the essential features of Paul's christology were already fully developed towards the end of the 40s, before the beginning of his great missionary journeys in the West. That means that there is less than twenty years available for the development of primitive Christian christology up to time [sic] of its earliest representative accessible to us, namely Paul."[26] Hengel notes that it is widely agreed that Jesus probably died in April of A.D. 30, and that Paul's conversion on the road to Damascus took place between A.D. 32 and 34.[27] Paul's letters were written between A.D. 50 and A.D. 57.

"However," Hengel further notes, "as we cannot detect any development in the basic christological views in his letters and furthermore he presupposes that the christological titles, forumulae and conceptions which he uses are known in the communities to which he is writing, so that they go back to the content of his mission preaching when he founded these communities,"[28] those views must have been firmly in place by the late 40s. That is an incredibly small window for major mythological developments. Within a space of some eighteen years or so, Paul emerged with a fully formed christology that contains many clear references to pre-Pauline language, titles, and theological assertions (such as, for instance, the great Christological hymn in Philippians 2:5–11). "In essentials,"

---

[26] Martin Hengel, *Between Jesus and Paul: Studies in the Earliest History of Christianity* (Philadelphia: Fortress Press, 1983), 31. In his endnotes to this section, Hengel writes: "Unfortunately too little attention is paid to the historical consequences of this 'shortage of time'" (p. 158).

[27] Most scholars date Paul's conversion between A.D. 32 and A.D. 38. Ben Witherington III gives A.D. 34/35 for his conversion in *The Paul Quest: The Renewed Search for the Jew of Tarsus* (Downers Grove, IL: IVP Press, 1998), 307. In Hengel's later book (written with Anna Maria Schwemer) *Paul Between Damascus and Antioch: The Unknown Years* (Louisville, KY: Westminster John Knox Press, 1997), the date of A.D. 33 is given (xi). The Catholic exegete Fr. Lucien Cerfaux gives the same date in *The Spiritual Journey of Saint Paul* (New York: Sheed and Ward, 1968), xvii.

[28] Hengel, *Between Jesus and Paul*, 31.

Hengel writes, "more happened in christology within these few years"—that is, from A.D. 32 to A.D. 50—"than in the whole subsequent seven hundred years of church history. Philippians 2:6ff., 1 Cor. 8:6, Gal. 4:4, Rom. 8:3 and 1 Cor. 2:7 already bear witness to the pre-existence and divine nature of Jesus and his mediation in creation."[29]

The numbers, in short, just don't add up to anything supporting the Myth Theory, despite attempts by some critics to fit the square peg of the theory into the round hole of the chronology. And so Hengel observes, rather dryly, "If we look through some works on the history of earliest Christianity we might get the impression that people in them had declared war on chronology."[30] The essential point that Hengel makes for our purposes here is the most logical explanation for these developments is not mythological manipulation but the real and transformative experiences of disciples who were witnesses, in one way or another, to the reality of the Resurrection of their Lord and Master. Closely related is the fact that if Paul was teaching something about the Resurrection of Christ that was contrary to what the other Apostles taught and the early Christian communities believed, we surely would see some overt evidence of conflict and disagreement.

Q. What light do the Gospels shed on the question of whether the Resurrection of Jesus was a later myth?

The Gospels make it even more improbable that the doctrine of Jesus's Resurrection was a later myth. Even assuming, for

---

[29] Ibid., 39–40.
[30] Ibid., 39.

the sake of argument, that no eyewitnesses wrote any of the four Gospels and that the Gospels appeared in the last quarter of the first century, in the second and third generations of Christians (forty to seventy years after the events they purport to depict), it is difficult to dismiss their accounts as myths. The Gospels themselves appear to pass along earlier tradition, tradition rooted in eyewitness accounts (*cf.* Lk 1:1–2; Jn 21:24–25). It is highly unlikely that the Gospel writers—and therefore Christian leaders who would have approved and circulated the Gospels—would have lost touch with the apostolic teaching on the nature of Jesus's Resurrection in such a short time. After all, the Death and Resurrection of Christ are the climatic events in all four Gospels, and take up substantial space in each.

The Resurrection of Jesus was a central Christian tenet, as we see in Paul's writings. It seems incredible, as noted already, that there could have been radical differences between what the Apostles and the next generation of Christian leaders believed and taught about it. It is hard to understand how the Gospel accounts could be widely accepted by the early Christian communities if those accounts describe things about Jesus deeply at odds with what the Apostles and others had passed on to the Christian communities. We would expect some lingering historical evidence of a profound upheaval on the point, and yet we see none. "Within earliest Christianity," Keener observes, "however, there remains no debate about the received tradition that Jesus himself rose bodily, unless one is inclined to count as proof inferences from silence offered by some modern scholars without explicit supporting evidence."[31]

---

[31] Keener, *The Historical Jesus of the Gospels*, 339.

Put another way: while plenty of modern scholars doubt or deny the physical Resurrection of Christ, it's impossible to dismiss the fact that the early Christians, without exception, accepted it and proclaimed it.

Q. What about the claim that the empty tomb story originated after A.D. 70—too late for it to be refuted by the authorities producing Jesus's corpse?

The argument assumes facts not in evidence—namely, that the empty tomb tradition originated only after A.D. 70. If we grant, for the sake of argument, that *all* the Gospels were written after A.D. 70, it doesn't follow that the empty tomb tradition doesn't go back to the beginning of Christianity. As we have seen, Paul and others proclaimed the bodily nature of the Resurrection long before A.D. 70. That preaching would have been sufficient to trigger a response in the Jewish authorities, if in fact they had the body of Jesus or knew where it was.

Q. How does the Myth Theory address the matter of the empty tomb?

The Myth Theory puts an interesting spin on the matter of the empty tomb, saying the empty tomb story supposedly originated *after* the fall of Jerusalem in A.D. 70—some forty years after Jesus's Death. By then, of course, it would have been too late for the Jewish authorities to refute Christian teaching by producing Jesus's corpse, even assuming anyone knew where it was buried.

Directly related to this point is that some critics are suspicious of the depiction of Joseph of Arimathea burying Jesus.

All four Gospels, as we've seen, credit Joseph with Jesus's burial. Certain critics claim that we can detect a gradual "Christianizing" of Joseph as the tradition of Jesus's burial developed: from a Jewish leader trying to do the right thing in burying Jesus, to a sympathetic non-Christian, to an actual (but secret) follower of Jesus. John Dominic Crossan argues that Mark's account of Joseph of Arimathea (*cf.* Mk 15:42–47) is "Mark's own creation";[32] he suggests that both Mark and Luke fabricated the new and unused tomb. Crossan says that Mark's story presents a "double dilemma": if Joseph "was in the council, he was against Jesus; if he was for Jesus, he was not in the council. Second, if Joseph buried Jesus from piety or duty, he would have done the same for the two other crucified criminals; yet if he did that, there could be no empty-tomb sequence." Thus, Crossan concludes that "Mark created that burial by Joseph of Arimathea in 15:42–47."[33]

The implication is that this process shows the burial by Joseph to be a legend concocted by the early Church to prove that Jesus's enemies buried him, rather than his disciples, who might have fabricated the Resurrection. And if the burial of Jesus is a legend, then so must be the empty tomb.

Q. So there are problems with the portrayal of Jesus's burial by Joseph of Arimathea?

As we have seen, some critics reject it on the grounds that we can supposedly see a "Christianizing tendency" in the story. From this they think it follows that if the Gospel accounts of Jesus's burial can be shown to have been embellished,

---

[32] John Dominic Crossan, *The Birth of Christianity* (San Francisco: HarperSanFrancisco, 1999), 554.
[33] Ibid., 555.

then they must be thrown out as altogether unreliable when it comes to evidence that the Jewish authorities and the Christians alike knew where Jesus was buried. And if the authorities and early Christians didn't know where Jesus was buried, then they could hardly have found his tomb empty.

First, even if the Joseph of Arimathea story were a later legend, it wouldn't follow that the empty tomb tradition must likewise be unhistorical or that the Jewish authorities wouldn't have known what happened to Jesus's body and therefore wouldn't have been able to refute claims of resurrection by producing it. Nor would it mean the early Christians didn't know what happened to Jesus's body. Only if we assume the authorities or the early Church didn't know where the body was buried or that the Christians didn't preach a bodily Resurrection can we get around the problem of why the Church wasn't stopped cold by the authorities producing Jesus's corpse. But, by itself, reducing the Joseph of Arimathea story to legend implies neither of those things.[34]

Do the Gospels manifest a Christianizing tendency when it comes to Joseph? It's doubtful, though possible. At most, we can say that there is a modest increase in detail regarding Joseph. Neither Mark nor Luke posits that Joseph was a *disciple* of Jesus; they say only that Joseph was "looking for the kingdom of God" (Mk 15:43; Lk 23:51). Matthew 27:57 and John 19:38 claim Joseph was a disciple, though John says he

---

[34] In fact, Crossan is decidedly in the minority in his rejection of the Marcan account of Joseph of Arimathea, the historical credibility of which "remains accepted by very many biblical scholars from Bultmann to Fitzmyer and beyond" (O'Collins, *Believing In the Resurrection*, Kindle eBook). Fitzmyer states that "in all four Gospels [Joseph of Arimathea] is linked to the burial of Jesus, clearly a historical reminiscence being used. Who would invent him?" (*The Gospel According Luke X-XXIV*, 1526).

was a secret disciple "for fear of the Jews." Did Matthew and John change Joseph from merely one seeking the kingdom into a full-blown disciple?

That's possible. But it's also possible they refer to Joseph as a disciple because he *later* became one, after the Resurrection. And it's possible Mark and Luke left out the fact Joseph was a disciple in order to avoid suggesting he had conspired with the disciples to steal the body. Another possibility is that Joseph was on the fence; he wasn't a full-fledged follower of Jesus and from that perspective couldn't really be called a disciple. Yet he may have been highly sympathetic to Jesus and his teaching and therefore something of a quasi-disciple.[35] This would answer Crossan's first point sufficiently. Mark and Luke may disqualify him from being a disciple using a stricter measure, while Matthew and John include him as a disciple, even if in a qualified sense in John's case, using a broader or less rigorous definition.

The point is, we simply don't know. We can't say, therefore, that the difference between Mark and Luke on the one hand and Matthew and John on the other reveals a Christianizing tendency over time. And even if Matthew and John did make Joseph into a disciple when in fact he wasn't one, does that mean they made him bury Jesus when he really didn't? Couldn't it just as well be said that they Christianized Joseph to account for the fact that he buried Jesus?

Q. Do we have other grounds for questioning the story of Jesus's burial by Joseph of Arimathea?

---

[35] Fitzmyer thinks Joseph is linked in Luke's Gospel "with the pious eschatologically-minded Jews of Jerusalem in the infancy narrative, Simeon (2:25) and Anna (2:38)" (*The Gospel According Luke X-XXIV*, 1527).

Not really. One argument is that Joseph's burial of Jesus conflicts with Acts 13:29, where Paul, addressing a synagogue,
attributes Jesus's burial to hostile Jewish leaders in Jerusalem,
whereas the Gospels have Jesus buried by a sympathetic, if
not believing, Joseph of Arimathea. But Acts 13:26–29 speaks
in general terms of many things the rulers of Jerusalem did
to Jesus. Consequently, when Paul says that "they . . . laid
him in a tomb," "they" could include Joseph, since he was a
member of the Sanhedrin, the Jewish council (*cf.* Mk 15:43;
Lk 23:50), and one of the rulers of Jerusalem. This view makes
even more sense if Joseph wasn't really a full-fledged follower
of Jesus at that time, but merely someone sympathetic to
his cause and who, as an act of righteousness, wanted to
ensure Jesus a proper burial. In any event, we have no serious
grounds for rejecting the claim that Joseph of Arimathea
buried Jesus. "This story is likely to be true," writes historian Michael Grant, "since the absence, which it records, of
any participation by Jesus's followers was too unfortunate,
indeed disgraceful, to have been voluntarily invented by the
evangelists at a later date."[36]

Furthermore, it seems unlikely that the early Christians,
given their hostility to the Jewish leadership, would fabricate
a story with a member of the Sanhedrin helping to bury Jesus,
if there were no basis in fact to it. And if, for some reason,
the early Christians wanted to fabricate a burial of Jesus by
Jewish leadership, why not pick the high priest rather than
a less significant unknown figure such as Joseph? Surely the
high priest would have more apologetical clout in such a role
than one Joseph of Arimathea.

---

[36] Michael Grant, *Jesus: An Historian's Review of the Gospels* (New York:
Charles Scribner's Sons, 1977), 175.

If, as some critics claim, it was Jesus's enemies, not a sympathetic Joseph of Arimathea, who buried Jesus, then we can suppose they knew where the body was. Which brings us back to the question of why they didn't produce the remains, once the Christians claimed Jesus had been raised. Since we have shown there is no reason to think the early Christians espoused anything other than a bodily Resurrection of Jesus, we have no reason to think that if the Christians' enemies had Jesus's body or knew where it was, they wouldn't have used it to undercut, if not completely refute, Christian claims of Jesus's Resurrection. The most reasonable conclusion to draw from the fact that the authorities did not produce Jesus's corpse or indicate what happened to it—apart from the story of the disciples' theft—is that they didn't have it or know where it was.

Q. What are the arguments against the Myth Theory?

First, as discussed, the Myth Theory fails because there isn't enough time for a resurrection myth to develop. Paul wrote in the 50s about of Jesus's Resurrection, within the first generation of Christians (A.D. 30–70). In doing so, he refers to the *common understanding* of Jesus and his teaching shared by the earliest witnesses. And this most certainly included Jesus's Resurrection.

In Galatians 1:18, for example, Paul describes how, three years after his conversion to Christianity (sometime in the mid to late 30s), he went to Jerusalem and conferred with Cephas (Peter) for fifteen days. Of this lengthy visit, Hengel and Schwemer surmise that Paul would have been "less concerned with personal information about Peter and his character than with his theological thought, more precisely christology and soteriology or—less abstractly—the content of his preaching, which certainly also included a narrative of Jesus's words and actions."[37] The author adds:

> In other words, Jesus above all else will have stood at the centre of the conversations—about six years after the Passover at which he died—the earthly and crucified, risen and exalted Jesus, who was now preached and was to come. For both Peter and Paul, his person and the salvation which he had achieved had become the centre of their lives.[38]

Had they not discussed this, Hengel and Schwemer propose, the visit would have been much shorter: "Since time was pressing, it would have been a pity to talk only about the weather."[39]

Paul also writes how he saw James, "the Lord's brother" (Gal 1:19). Is it reasonable to think Paul did not discuss Jesus's Resurrection with them? Or to believe that if they had a different understanding of Jesus's post-mortem appearances, this difference wouldn't have come up in conversation? The most reasonable conclusion to draw is that within six or eight years of Jesus's Death, Paul understood what others held about Jesus—he had been *resurrected*. And that this Resurrection involved Jesus being raised into a transformed kind of bodily existence.

Fourteen years after his initial meeting with Peter and James, Paul returned to Jerusalem and presented his teaching to Peter, James, and John (*cf.* Gal 2:1–2, 9). According to Paul, they unreservedly recognized the authenticity of his teaching (*cf.* Gal 2:6–7, 9–10). Again, it seems unreasonable

---

[37] Hengel and Schwemer, *Paul Between Damascus and Antioch*, 146.
[38] Ibid., 147.
[39] Ibid.

to think Paul's understanding of Jesus's fate—Resurrection—can have differed significantly from the view of Peter, James, and John. It's difficult to imagine he would cite them in support of his orthodoxy if he knew they believed something very different about the central teaching concerning Jesus. And in 1 Corinthians 15:3–14, which we will discuss below, Paul justifies his teaching about the future resurrection of Christians by appealing to Jesus's Resurrection, which he argues has been vouchsafed by the witnesses. It would have been absurd for Paul to appeal to their testimony if he knew they held a different idea of what happened to Jesus. The earliest leaders of the Jesus Movement, then, taught the Resurrection of Jesus. There are no reasonable grounds for regarding this as a later idea or a myth.

Two more quick points: 1) As touched on before, there is the fact that the first witnesses were women, whose testimony would have been considered worthless. "If, on the other hand, the writers were simply reporting what they saw, they would have to tell the truth, however socially and legally inconvenient."[40] 2) Paul, in his First Letter to Timothy, exhorts the younger man: "Have nothing to do with godless and silly myths" (1 Tm 4:7). And the second epistle of Peter, again, strongly asserts: "For we did not follow cleverly devised myths when we made known to you the power and coming of our Lord Jesus Christ, but we were eyewitnesses of his majesty" (2 Pt 1:16). Paul and Peter apparently knew the difference between fact and myth. If either man had promoted a mythology, we would have to wonder—going

---

[40] Peter J. Kreeft and Ronald K. Tacelli, *Handbook of Catholic Apologetics: Reasoned Answers to Questions of Faith* (San Francisco: Ignatius Press, 2009), 204.

back to the Conspiracy Theory—*why*? What did either man have to gain? Neither man gained power or wealth, and both men were eventually executed in Rome for their belief in Christ. So, again, natural explanations do not provide convincing answers.

Chapter 8

The Apostle Paul and the Resurrection

Q. In 1 Corinthians 15, Paul corrects what he regards as certain Corinthian Christians' mistake about Jesus's Resurrection. Did the earliest Christians believe something different from the later Christians, including Paul? Apparently they didn't believe in the Resurrection of Jesus, even though they were Christians. Doesn't this suggest that something besides resurrection may have happened to Jesus after his Death?

Belief in Jesus's Resurrection isn't really at issue in Paul's discussion with the Corinthians. It's not as if the Corinthians didn't believe Jesus rose from the dead but Paul does. They all agreed about Jesus's Resurrection. Paul's argument is over the resurrection of *Christians* in the *future*, which some Corinthians apparently questioned. Paul said to them, in effect, "If there's no resurrection of the dead, as some of you believe, then Jesus himself hasn't been raised from the dead. And if that's true, then we're in trouble—our faith is worthless and we're still in our sins. But we *know* Christ has been resurrected. The witnesses confirm this—Peter, all of the Twelve, the five hundred witnesses, James, the other Apostles, and me. So we know there will be a resurrection of the dead for us, too."

Paul used Jesus's Resurrection, in which the Corinthians also believed, in order to argue for the future resurrection of

Christians, which *some* Corinthians apparently questioned. "Some of the Corinthians dispute the future resurrection of believers," explains Craig Keener. "They cannot, however, dispute the past resurrection of Jesus, because this is an established fact and the very foundation of their faith. Yet Paul points out that this fact cannot be separated from the future resurrection of believers (15:12–14)."[1] In other words, Paul argues *from* Jesus's Resurrection more than *for* it in 1 Corinthians 15. He argues *from* Jesus's Resurrection, which his readers accept, *to* the idea of the resurrection of Christians, which some question.[2] Paul said nothing, as such, about different understandings of Jesus's Resurrection among the Corinthians.

Still, suppose he did. Let's suppose there were a group of early Christians who thought of Jesus as, say, a disembodied spirit. Why should we suppose such an idea would represent an *earlier* understanding of Jesus's after-death state? Why couldn't such a view be a distortion of the original Christian belief? There is no evidence that the Corinthian Christians thought of Jesus as a disembodied spirit, but even if they had it wouldn't mean their idea came first and Paul's was a later notion rather than the other way around.

----

[1]   Craig S. Keener, *The IVP Bible Background Commentary: New Testament* (Downers Grove, IL: IVP Academic, 1993), 484.

[2]   "By adding his instruction on the resurrection, Paul suggests that the Christians in Corinth would not have experienced so many problems and conflicts if they had understood—or better, if they had really accepted—the ramifications of the resurrection of the body. Almost all the Corinthians' misunderstandings were related to their failure to correctly appreciate the physical. All Christian faith depends upon acceptance of the reality of the resurrection (15:1–11)." Mary Ann Getty, R.S.M., *First Corinthians and Second Corinthians: Collegeville Bible Commentary* (Collegeville, MN: The Liturgical Press, 1983), 70.

Q. Paul describes his encounter with the risen Jesus as a "vision" (*cf.* Acts 9:1–9, 22:6–11, 26:12–18). Since Paul claims his encounter was the same *kind* of event as other Apostles' meetings with Jesus, they, too, must have seen a vision. But a vision isn't the same as meeting a resurrected being, so doesn't this implies Jesus's body remained in the tomb?

This argument puts too much weight on the word vision. There are several important things to note. Paul insists that a *resurrected* Jesus appeared to him as well as to others, including the disciples. He doesn't say that the exact manner of encounter was the same in all cases, but he insists Jesus was the same—the resurrected Jesus.

Furthermore, Paul himself doesn't use the word vision in his writings to describe his meeting with Jesus. It is Luke's summary of Paul's account, recorded in Acts 26:19, that speaks of Paul having a vision of Jesus. We shouldn't suppose the summary necessarily uses Paul's own exact wording. According to 1 Corinthians 15:8, Paul saw the risen Jesus but he doesn't refer to this as a vision: "Last of all, as to one untimely born, he appeared also to me."

For Luke, Jesus's Resurrection appearances generally ceased with the Ascension of Jesus into Heaven (*cf.* Acts 1:6–11), where he stands "at the right hand of God" (Acts 7:56). Paul's encounter is an exception. In all cases, Luke clearly regards the resurrected Jesus as an embodied being. For example, Jesus assures the disciples he is not a spirit, but a bodily being with flesh and bones (*cf.* Lk 24:39–40). He even eats before them (Lk 24:41–43).[3] Even if Luke intends to describe Paul's

---

[3] "Only Luke among the evangelists indulges in this sort of realism about the existence of the risen Christ," remarks Fr. Joseph Fitzmyer, SJ, "and for this he is castigated, by twentieth-century readers! In 20:27–29 John as an

encounter with the resurrected Jesus as in some way a vision, Luke still understands it to be a vision of a resurrected being, a bodily being. Fr. Joseph A. Fitzmyer in his two-volume commentary on the Gospel of Luke notes,

> Indeed, Luke strives explicitly (24:37–39) to dispel the idea that Christ was like a spook or a shot, insisting on the reality of his risen person, portraying him eating broiled fish, and stressing that his body experienced no decay (Acts 2:27, 13:35, 37).... The primitive kerygma, which affirmed Jesus' resurrection from the dead, was formulated in Palestine and in a culture which would have scarcely been able to conceive of anything but a "bodily" resurrection.[4]

In other words, Luke doesn't regard Paul's vision to mean Jesus's body was still in the tomb or that Paul spoke to Jesus's spirit. For Luke, Paul can meet Jesus on the road to Damascus (*cf.* Acts 9:3–7) because Jesus rose from the dead, which, as Luke understands it, means the tomb is empty and the corpse of Jesus has been transformed (*cf.* Lk 24:5–6). It is instructive here to keep in mind Fr. Fitzmyer's explanation that the Resurrection of Christ

> is called in question in modern times because of attempts to square it with the dichotomy of body and soul inherited from Greek philosophy and common to all modern western thought.... Denials

---

evangelist has his own way of stressing the reality, yet he is rarely castigated in the same way." *The Gospel According to Luke X-XXIV: The Anchor Bible* (Garden City, NY: Doubleday & Company, Inc., 1986), 1577.

[4]   Ibid., 1538–39. Keener points out that "[a]ll our early Christian sources unanimously affirm the bodily resurrection of Jesus, although 1 Cor 15 attests that Paul had to deal with some Gentile Christians who could assimilate the Palestinian Jewish doctrine only with difficulty and did not wish to accept it beyond the case of Jesus.... Within early Christianity, however, there remains no debate about the received tradition that Jesus himself rose bodily, unless one is inclined to count as proof inferences from silence offered by some modern scholars without explicit supporting evidence" (*The Historical Jesus in the Gospels*, 339).

of the "resurrection" were current already in Paul's time (as 1 Corinthians 15 attests), but not even he was trying to cope with the modern problems.[5]

If we accept the Lord's appearance to Paul in 1 Corinthians 15:8 to be the same as his vision of Jesus as recounted by Luke in Acts 9:3–7, then we must accept that the latter *also implies an empty tomb*. We can't argue from the supposedly visionary nature of Paul's encounter with the risen Lord to a conclusion that the body of Jesus was still in the tomb.

In 1 Corinthians 15:8, Paul claims to have seen the same risen Lord the other Apostles saw,[6] not a ghost or an apparition of a dead person. He doesn't use the word vision to describe the experience but instead speaks of Jesus appearing to him as he appeared to the other witnesses of the Resurrection. The fact that Paul regards the others and himself as all seeing the risen Jesus doesn't rule out some differences between how he encountered Jesus and how the others did, but it does preclude any difference in Jesus himself. In all cases—Paul seeing the Lord and the others seeing him—Jesus himself is the same: resurrected from the dead. For Paul, that means Jesus is no longer "buried" (1 Cor 15:4), which means the tomb was empty.

Q. Didn't Stephen, the first Christian martyr, have a vision of the triumphant Jesus in Heaven? Couldn't Paul's vision be the same sort of thing?

There are two things to consider here. Before Stephen died, he saw a vision of the triumphant Jesus: "I see... the Son of

---

[5] Fitzmyer, *The Gospel According to Luke X-XXIV*, 1539–40.
[6] "Have I not seen Jesus our Lord?" (1 Cor 9:1).

Man standing at the right hand of God" (Acts 7:56). But the description of Stephen's vision only serves to distinguish it from Paul's encounter. In Stephen's vision, Jesus is said to be *in Heaven*; whereas in Paul's encounter, it isn't stated that Jesus is in Heaven. There's a light from "heaven" (*cf.* Acts 9:3), or the sky, but it doesn't say that Paul saw Jesus in Heaven (*cf.* Acts 9:3–8, 22:6–11, 26:12–18). In Acts 26:19, Paul refers to this as a "heavenly vision," but that refers to the *source* of the encounter, not where he *saw* Jesus. Also, while the men with Paul do not see Jesus or understand his words, they hear a voice (*cf.* Acts 9:7) and see the light (*cf.* Acts 22:9). These details imply that Luke intends us to understand the encounter as an objective event, even if an extraordinary one. Subjective visions (and hallucinations, as we've noted) aren't usually shared.

Also, why would Paul, a Pharisee, interpret a vision of the triumphant spirit of Jesus as a resurrection? A vision of a dead man, even a vindicated one, wouldn't of itself lead a Pharisee such as Paul to conclude that the dead man had been resurrected; Paul would more likely think he had seen a spirit or experienced a sort of theophany.[7] As we have seen, resurrection was something Pharisaic Jews such as Paul thought will happen at the *end* of the world, to all the righteous, not in the course of history. Unless Paul was convinced something miraculous had happened to Jesus's body, it seems highly unlikely he would have spoken of Jesus's

---

[7] "Light or lightning is a regular feature of theophanies in the Bible (*cf.* Exod. 19:6; 2 Sam. 22:15), but here we are talking about a Christophany." Ben Witherington III, *The Acts of the Apostles: A Socio-Rhetorical Commentary* (Grand Rapids, MI: William B. Eerdmans Publishing Company, 1998), 316. Witherington notes that the language used by Luke clearly indicates he "is comfortable using the language of divinity of the exalted Christ" (p. 316).

Resurrection on the basis of a mere vision. And then there is the time that Paul spent with Peter and other early Church leaders, discussing what they had seen and experienced, and more deeply forming his theological understanding of the life, Death, and Resurrection of Jesus.

Q. You cite Paul in support of the empty tomb but he nowhere mentions it. The Gospels first mention the empty tomb—and they were written much later than when Paul wrote of Jesus's Death in 1 Corinthians 15. Doesn't this indicate the idea of an empty tomb was a later invention?

To claim that Paul doesn't mention the empty tomb is misleading. He doesn't *explicitly* mention the empty tomb, but he does quote an early Christian source—apparently an early Christian creedal statement—that Jesus was *buried* and raised (*cf.* 1 Cor 15:4). This implies that wherever his body had been buried, it wasn't there anymore as result of the Resurrection. Davis states:

> Paul's own view of the nature of the resurrection, in my opinion, *requires* that the tomb be empty (which is the reversal of what is sometimes claimed). This is because his simile of the plant growing from the seed (*cf.* 1 Cor 15:35–43) entails material continuity between the one and the other. That is to say, Paul's view would seem to imply that Jesus's body could not be still decomposing in the tomb, because it had been transformed into—it *became*—Jesus's Resurrection body (just as the seed becomes the plant).[8]

The same idea seems evident in Paul's Letter to the Romans: "If the Spirit of him who raised Jesus from the dead dwells in you, he who raised Christ Jesus from the dead will give life to

---

[8]   Davis, *Risen Indeed*, 76; emphasis in original.

your mortal bodies also through his Spirit who dwells in you" (Rom 8:11).

While Paul doesn't use the word tomb, he does refer to Jesus's burial, which implies a burial site or grave site. That Jesus was buried and is no long buried but raised is the essence of the empty tomb story, so we can say that Paul explicitly affirms the main point of the empty tomb account, even if he doesn't use the words "empty tomb." Paul certainly didn't think Jesus remained buried; in fact, he may well have not mentioned the tomb directly because what he believed and taught about the Resurrection entailed an empty tomb— it was simply a given—and because "the witnesses provide stronger proof of what happened to Jesus ([1 Cor] 15:5–8)."[9]

Q. When Paul refers to Jesus's burial (*cf.* 1 Cor 15:4), doesn't he simply mean that Jesus died? Why should we see Paul's statement as implying his knowledge of the empty tomb?

The preceding clause of the statement unambiguously asserted that Jesus died: "Christ died for our sins in accordance with the scriptures" (1 Cor 15:3). The statement that "he was buried" is part of a sequence of events—Death, burial, Resurrection, and appearances—not merely an amplification of the previous assertion of Jesus's Death. For Paul, Jesus died, was buried, was raised from the dead, and appeared to various people, including Paul himself. There is a progression of things the embodied Jesus did—died, was buried, rose from the dead, and encountered people.

Craig has shown that these four events—Death, burial, Resurrection, and appearances—directly correlate to the

---

[9]   Keener, *The IVP Bible Background Commentary*, 484.

four events described in Acts 13:28–31 and Mark 15:37–16:8. His point, in part, is that when Paul wrote, "He was buried" (1 Cor 15:4), it corresponds directly to the statements "they took him down from the tree, and laid him in a tomb" (Acts 13:29) and "taking him down, wrapped him in the linen shroud, and laid him in a tomb" (Mk 15:46). "When Paul quoted those old sayings," Craig notes, "he knew the broader context that the saying summarized. (Look, for example, at his detailed knowledge of Jesus's words at the Last Supper as Paul records them in 1 Corinthians 11:23–26.)"[10] Surely he would have discussed this point during his two-week-long visit with Peter!

Burial, then, is much more than a generic reference to the fact of Jesus's Death. It describes what happened to his body after death. Jesus's being "raised on the third day" (1 Cor 15:4) refers to what happened after he was buried. It means he is no longer buried but is now raised. At least that's how Paul saw it. And, as we have seen, Paul knew the earliest witnesses to the Death, burial, and Resurrection of Jesus—among them Cephas (Peter), the Twelve (the first group of leaders among Jesus's followers), and James (*cf.* 1 Cor 15:3–7). It is unlikely Paul would cite them in support of his argument for the Resurrection if they held a different view of Jesus's burial and Resurrection from Paul.

Q. As you noted, many scholars regard the list of witnesses cited by Paul as something like an earlier creedal statement. Could it be that Paul simply repeats it without any direct knowledge himself of what it implies about Jesus's burial and the empty tomb?

---

[10] Craig, *The Son Rises*, 49–50.

That's highly unlikely, given that Paul once persecuted the Church (*cf.* 1 Cor 15:9; Gal 1:13) and so would have in all likelihood investigated Christian claims regarding Jesus, including claims of his burial. It is hard to imagine that Paul never investigated the matter as he opposed the early Christians.

After his conversion Paul met the Jerusalem leaders of the early Church, as we saw (*cf.* Gal 1:18, 2:1–10). Just as it is unlikely Paul would have ignored the chance to ask Peter, James, and John and others about Jesus's Resurrection appearances, it is unlikely he would pass on the opportunity to confirm the details of Jesus's Death and burial. We have good reason to suppose, then, Paul is doing more than uncritically repeating a primitive creedal statement.

Q. But doesn't it seem as if Paul didn't require belief in the empty tomb in order to believe in the risen Jesus?

That statement is also misleading, if only because it appears to assume that a reference to the empty tomb is absolutely necessary. Paul, however, didn't require explicit mention of the empty tomb in order to believe in the Resurrection, but he did require belief in the *essence* of the empty tomb story—that Jesus died, was buried, and was raised. Since Jesus couldn't have been buried and raised, as Paul understands the notion of Resurrection, without the body of Jesus leaving the place where it had been buried, it follows that Paul requires the gist of the empty tomb story—that Jesus's body is no longer buried—in order for one to believe in Jesus's Resurrection. N. T. Wright writes,

> It is vital to grasp that for a Pharisee of Paul's background and training the resurrection meant, inalienably and incontestably, the

bodily resurrection. 1 Corinthians 15 rules out two possible ways of understanding the resurrection. On the one hand, Paul didn't see it as simply the resuscitation of a corpse. Jesus didn't return to the same mode of physical existence as he had lived before. On the other hand, Paul didn't see it as the abandonment of Jesus's physical body. If you had suggested to him that 'the resurrection' might have occurred while the tomb of Jesus was still occupied by his corpse, he wouldn't have just disagreed; he would have suggested that you didn't understand what the relevant words meant.[11]

Furthermore, it would be superfluous to mention explicitly the empty tomb in 1 Corinthians 15:4. The point of mentioning the empty tomb would be to show that Jesus was no longer dead; his corpse is no longer there because he was raised from where he was buried. But Paul's argument is that he and others have *seen* the risen Lord. Paul doesn't need to appeal to the empty tomb; he can appeal to his and others' direct experience of encountering the risen Jesus, even though his appeal tacitly assumes, by the nature of the event appealed to, the essence of the empty tomb story: Jesus is no longer buried where he was because he has been raised from the dead.

---

[11] Wright, *What Saint Paul Really Said*, 50.

Chapter 9

Physical and Spiritual

Q. The Gospels go out of their way to say the risen Jesus isn't a spirit. Doesn't this imply that *some* early Christians espoused the earlier, non-bodily Resurrection view and the Gospels are trying to refute it?

The Gospel accounts may suggest some controversy about the bodily nature of Jesus's Resurrection, but this doesn't mean there was a group of *Christians* who affirmed the Resurrection in some non-bodily or purely spiritual sense.[1] Luke 24:36–43, for example, clearly wants to refute the idea that the disciples saw

---

[1]   Lüdemann argues that while Paul held to a strong belief in the bodily resurrection (despite having hallucinated his encounter with Christ), early forms of Gnosticism—notably Docetism, which held that Jesus only appeared to have a body—began to infiltrate the thinking of some Christians, especially Gentile converts. "Lüdemann contends that the resurrection narratives in the canonical Gospels were created later, in response to challenges such as the symbolic interpretation and Docetism" (*The Resurrection of Jesus*, 503). Licona further points out, in rather blunt fashion, that Lüdemann "projects his own antisupernatural bias onto the first-century theists in a demeaning manner" (p. 512). Yet, Licona adds, "without a single known exception, all of the original apostolic leaders and all of the relevant Christian literature strongly believed to have been written in the first century are of a single voice in their proclamation that Jesus had been raised bodily" (p. 514). In other words, if the Evangelists and Paul did respond to an anti-physical Resurrection position, it was to ideas coming from outside the Christian movement.

a ghost. Does that mean some early Christians believed Jesus appeared as a ghost? We have no more reason to think so, simply because of the passage from Luke's Gospel than we have to think some Christians believed the disciples stole Jesus's body because of Matthew 28:15. It is more reasonable to think Luke has in mind non-Christians, whether Jews or Gentiles, rather than Christian proponents of a supposedly more primitive, spiritual resurrection. Surely non-Christians would have argued against early Christian claims about the Resurrection appearances by trying to explain them as ghost stories. That is reason enough for why Resurrection accounts refuting the idea would be recounted.

But, for the sake of argument, let's grant the premise and suppose some Christians living when the Gospels were written did hold to a spiritual resurrection idea. Why shouldn't we see them as influenced by Gnostics of a later day, rather than as stalwarts of an earlier, spiritualized view of the Resurrection? Gnostics had a deep disdain for the material world; they and those influenced by them tended to deny the reality of Jesus's humanity.[2] It is much easier to fit the Gospel emphasis on Jesus's humanity—including his humanity before the Resurrection— with the idea of Christianity encountering and responding to Gnosticism, than with supposedly primitive Christian advocates of spiritual resurrection. For Gnostics to believe in Jesus in any sense, they had to undercut—if not deny outright—the bodily nature of the Resurrection, especially if the Resurrection was regarded by them as an exaltation to the divine.

In fact, we know Gnostic-influenced Christians sometimes even denied Jesus's Death (which we shouldn't interpret as

---

2   Docetism, an early form of Gnosticism, is derived from the Greek word "*dokeīn*," which means "to seem" or "to appear"—that is, Jesus only *seemed* or *appeared* to be human.

residual of an early, alternative Christian regarding Jesus's fate), because they rejected the goodness and reality of the physical realm. We can, therefore, explain a belief in a non-physical resurrection, if that's what the Gospels are responding to, as a Gnostic or Gnostic-influenced distortion of the primitive, Jewish Christian proclamation rather than as a hold-over of some alleged primitive, visionary notion of Resurrection, for which there is no evidence. The early tendency towards a docetist, Gnostic understanding of Jesus likely existed in the first century and was apparently addressed in some of the later writings of Paul (Colossians and the pastoral epistles) and John (*cf.* 1 Jn 4:2, 5:6; 2 Jn 1:7).[3] It makes more sense to think Gnosticism distorted a more primitive, Jewish Christian understanding of the Resurrection than to allege a primitive spiritual-Jesus-whose-body-is-still-in-the-tomb notion of the Resurrection later carnalized in the doctrine of the bodily resurrection.

What evidence we have of Christian controversy with Gnosticism on the point situates that controversy towards the end of the first century, not in the first half and middle of the century, which is when Paul and the others proclaimed the Resurrection. We have no evidence of an alternative understanding of the Resurrection at that early date, not even a Gnostic one; those came later, in the second century.

Q. What is the Spiritual Resurrection Theory?

This is the idea that the Resurrection of Jesus was purely spiritual and not at all corporeal or bodily. The risen Jesus was a spirit. Those who encountered him encountered the spirit

---

[3]   Keener, *The IVP Bible Background Commentary*, 825.

of Jesus. His corpse is irrelevant, in this view. Whether dogs ate it[4] or it remains buried in a tomb makes no difference. Jesus's body wasn't transformed; he was raised a spirit.

Q. Who advocates the idea of the Spiritual Resurrection Theory?

Some theologically liberal Christians espouse the Spiritual Resurrection Theory, or a form of it. It is held by John Shelby Spong, John Dominic Crossan, and Marcus Borg,[5] among others. Jehovah's Witnesses, oddly enough, also advocate a form of it. They think the various Resurrection appearances recounted in the New Testament do not reflect Jesus's actual resurrected state, but involve various bodies he assumed or materialized in order to indicate to his disciples his continued existence as a spirit.

Unlike most people who reject the traditional understanding of Jesus's Resurrection, advocates of the Spiritual Resurrection Theory generally appeal to the New Testament

---

[4] "The Dogs Beneath the Cross" is an entire chapter in John Dominic Crossan's *Jesus: A Revolutionary Biography* (San Francisco: HarperSanFrancisco, 1995), 123–58.

[5] Borg, who died in 2015, indicated that he thought the "spiritual/ physical" distinction is unhelpful and misleading. In an October 2013 blog post he wrote: "In I Corinthians 15 in which Paul not only affirms that the resurrection of Jesus as essential . . . he also says near the end of the chapter that the resurrected body is not physical but spiritual – a glorified body. What that means I do not know – but Paul contrasts it to a body of flesh and blood. I think it is doubtful that Paul can be cited as an authority for a material physical bodily resurrection.

"So also I do not think that the gospel stories of Easter require us to think of the resurrection in material physical terms. I see them as parables of the resurrection. Parables are about meaning. They are truth-filled and truthful stories, even as they may not be literally factual." ("Continuing the Resurrection Conversation," Oct 9, 2013, http://www.patheos.com/blogs/marcusborg/2013/10/continuing-the-resurrection-conversation/).

to support their views. As a result, the case against the theory involves a careful review of certain New Testament passages.

Q. Apparently, Jesus appeared to two disciples in "another form" (Mk 16:12). Doesn't this suggest that Jesus's bodily appearances are matters of convenience and that his true resurrection nature is a spirit?

Just because Jesus's appeared in different forms to the disciples doesn't mean he was a spirit. Perhaps one quality of a resurrected body is the capacity to manifest itself in different forms, while still retaining the underlying reality of a body. On the other hand, it may be that Mark 16:12 is a less precise way of saying that the disciples were miraculously kept from recognizing Jesus, as in Luke 24:16.[6] In either case, nothing requires us to think the resurrected Jesus became a disembodied spirit. A key issue here is continuity—not just Jesus's spirit before and after his Resurrection, but also his body. To acknowledge that Jesus's body has changed—has been glorified—is not the same as saying it is no longer a body.

Q. Paul refers to the resurrection body as a *spiritual body*. He writes, "It is sown a physical body, it is raised a spiritual body" (1 Cor 15:44). Doesn't this mean that Paul supports the Spiritual Resurrection Theory?

Paul states that the resurrected body is a spiritual body but this isn't the same thing as a spirit or the idea of *spiritual resurrection*. He contrasts what is sometimes translated as a

---

[6] Apparently, the appearance to the two disciples in Mark 16:12 is the same as Jesus's encounter of two disciples on the road to Emmaus (*cf.* Lk 24:13–35).

"physical body" to the "spiritual body" of the Resurrection. Because Paul's language here is easily misunderstood, we must carefully examine it.

Paul refers in 1 Corinthians 15:44 to "*soma psuchikon*" and "*soma pneumatikon*," to use the original Greek terms. These terms are sometimes translated, respectively, as "physical body" and "spiritual body." But that can be misleading, especially with respect to "physical body." Literally, the terms mean "soulish body" and "spiritual body."

In 1 Corinthians 15, Paul writes about the future resurrection of believers. He contrasts *mortal* existence of this life with *immortal* existence of the resurrection to come. In both cases, he refers to *bodily* existence. Notice he writes about a spiritual *body*, not simply a *spirit*. He contrasts two kinds of bodies: one subject to death, the other not subject to death. From this, some people wrongly conclude that *any* kind of *physical body* is necessarily a *mortal body*. Since, as Paul teaches, resurrected bodies are *spiritual bodies* (*soma pneumatikon*) and are immortal, some readers jump to the conclusion that resurrected bodies can't in any sense be physical.

But *soma psuchikon* does not mean *physical body*, as we generally understand the term physical. It would be more accurate to translate it as "natural body," since *psuchikon* here means "soulish" and refers to earthly or natural life, or life "animated by the soul" (*psuche* in Greek means "soul"). *Soma pneumatikon*, on the other hand, means "spiritual body" in the sense of "animated by spirit" or "animated by the Spirit"—rather than in the sense of being "a spirit" or a body "made out of spirit" (*pneuma* in Greek means "spirit").

Thus, Paul is contrasting two kinds of bodily life: the merely natural bodily life of mortal existence and the supernatural bodily life bestowed by the Spirit, which is an immortal existence. He isn't contrasting physicality as such with the spiritual, understood as immaterial.

That this is how Paul uses the terms "*psuchikon*" and "*pneumatikon*" can be seen by how he refers to the "natural man" or "unspiritual man" (*psuchikos anthropos*) and the "spiritual man" (*pneumatikos anthropos*) in 1 Corinthians 2:14–15. The natural man or naturally minded person is not a physical being in contrast to the spiritual man or spiritually minded person, who is a spirit. Both the "natural man" and the "spiritual man" are physical beings, with bodies of flesh and blood. The difference is that the naturally minded person (or natural man) is the "soulish" person, one who lives only according his natural, earthly impulses; whereas the spiritually minded person is someone who lives according to the supernatural, heavenly guidance of the Spirit.

Similarly, the "natural body" (a more accurate translation than "physical body") to which Paul refers in 1 Corinthians 15:44 is the body animated by the natural life of the human soul, while the "spiritual body" is the body animated by the spiritual life of God. Both bodies are physical in the sense that they're bodies and have the properties characteristic of bodies. But the resurrected body, the "spiritual body," is animated by the Spirit. Among other things, that makes it immortal, but it remains a body, not a spirit. In the words of Fr. Cerfaux:

> There is nothing to prevent the body from becoming an organ of the Spirit, and it can share in the Spirit's religious qualities such as incorruptibility or glory. The "spiritualized" body will not be completely different from the natural body, for the resurrected body will spring from the body which was buried in the earth. The mortal body, without being completely destroyed, will be raised to a higher rank, and the moral element will be swallowed up in life (2 Cor. 5:4).

> Thus the body of Christ, which came forth out of the tomb and was not annihilated.[7]

So, we must reject the Spiritual Resurrection Theory, which denies that the resurrected Jesus was embodied, because Paul speaks of the Resurrection involving a special kind of *bodily* life—a bodily life animated by the Spirit, to be sure, but still a form of bodily life. "When Paul talks about a 'spiritual body' (1 Corinthians 15:44)," states Wright, "he doesn't mean 'spiritual' in the Platonic sense, i.e., non-material. He means a *body* (physical, in some sense), which is *constituted* by 'spirit.'"[8]

Q. That's a bit bewildering! Can you clarify what you mean by *bodily* resurrection?

In a certain sense, to refer to *bodily* resurrection is redundant. It's like speaking of cold ice. Jewish notions of resurrection—ideas that would have been shared by Jesus and his disciples—were inherently *bodily*. To speak of resurrection was to talk about a bodily kind of existence.

Another way to consider the issue is to ask what we mean when we call something a "body." To be a "body" implies extension in space, size, a certain density, etc. These are attributes of *physical* things. A spiritual body, if it is in fact a "body," would, on this account, also be *physical* in this sense, since to be a "body" at all means to possess certain *physical* attributes.

We might imagine that a *spiritual* body would be able to do things *natural* bodies cannot do. For example, a spiritual body might be able to suspend those aspects of its bodily reality that would make it impossible to enter a sealed room, as Jesus

---

[7]   Cerfaux, *The Christian in the Theology of St. Paul*, 184–85.
[8]   Wright, *What Saint Paul Really Said*, 50.

is reported to have done (*cf.* Jn 20:19). Or a spiritual body might be capable of shape shifting, so to speak, so that it could alter its appearance, as Jesus may have done with the disciples on the road to Emmaus. Another possibility: a spiritual body might be able to move instantaneously from one location to another, without passing through the intervening space, as Jesus apparently did when he appeared to Saul of Tarsus from out of nowhere (*cf.* Act 9:3–6). But none of these things amounts to altering the essentially *physicality* of a body. A spiritual body may involve a different kind of physicality from a natural body, but it would still involve physicality by virtue of being a body.

Some scholars try to avoid confusion by speaking of the resurrection body as transphysical.[9] By this they mean resurrection bodies have traits we associate with physical bodies, but they also can behave in ways ordinary physical bodies can't. Whether we speak of the resurrected Jesus as having a physical body or a transphysical body, we should know he was not a mere spirit.

---

[9]   " 'Transphysical' is not meant to describe in detail what sort of body it was that the early Christians supposed Jesus already had, and believed that they themselves would eventually have. Nor indeed does it claim to explain how such a thing can come to be. It merely, but I hope usefully, puts a label on the demonstrable fact that the early Christians envisaged a body which was still robustly physical but also significantly different from the present one. If anything—since the main difference they seem to have envisaged is that the new body will not be corruptible—we might say not that it will be less physical, as though it were some kind of ghost or apparition, but more. 'Not unclothed, but more fully clothed.' . . . [The early Christians] were not talking about a non-bodily, 'spiritual' survival. Had they wanted to do so, they had plenty of other language available to them, as indeed we do today" (Wright, *The Resurrection of the Son of God*, 477–78).

Q. But doesn't Paul say that "flesh and blood cannot inherit the kingdom of God" (1 Cor 15:50)? Doesn't he mean by that *bodily life*?

A careful reading of the text shows that by "flesh and blood" Paul means flesh and blood as presently constituted—mortal and perishable bodies, i.e., "earthly life" or "mortal existence" (*cf.* Mt 16:17). He doesn't deny that the resurrected body of Jesus had flesh and blood in some fashion. His point is that the perishable does not inherit the imperishable (*cf.* 1 Cor 15:50, 53–4).

Elsewhere the New Testament teaches that the resurrected Jesus had flesh and blood—at least of some kind. In Luke 24:39, Jesus tells the disciples to touch him and see that he is no spirit, "for a spirit has not flesh and bones as you see that I have."

According to Hebrews 9:12, Jesus entered Heaven with "his own blood." As the high priest entered the Most Holy Place with the blood of the sacrifice, so Jesus entered Heaven, the true Tabernacle, with his own blood. Jesus's blood was shed on the Cross, but it was offered in Heaven through his resurrected presence before God, as the sacrificial blood was shed outside the Holy of Holies but was brought inside by the high priest. The implication is that sacrificed body and blood of Jesus are present in Heaven in the person of the risen, glorified Lord, who was both the priest who offered and the sacrifice offered, and who continues to make intercession for us before God.

Q. Paul also says that the "first Adam became a living being," quoting Genesis 2:7, while the last Adam, Jesus, became "a life-giving spirit" (1 Cor 15:45). Doesn't this suggest that the risen Jesus was a spirit?

The text doesn't say that Jesus was raised from the dead as a life-giving spirit. It states, "Thus it is written, 'The first man Adam became a living being'; the last Adam became a life-giving spirit. But it is not the spiritual which is first but the physical, and then the spiritual (1 Cor 15:45–46).

This refers to Jesus becoming the *source* of spiritual life because of his Resurrection. Paul also refers to the Spirit of God as the Spirit of Jesus (*cf.* Rom 8:9; Gal 4:6). Jesus is the one through whom the Father sends the Holy Spirit (*cf.* Jn 1:33, 7:39, 14:16, 26; Acts 1:4–5) and the Holy Spirit is the principle source of our life in Christ (*cf.* Rom 8:2). In 1 Corinthians 15:45 Paul says that as Adam was the source of our soulish life, or *natural life*, because he became a living soul or "a living being" as the biological progenitor of the race, so Jesus is the source of our *spiritual life*, since his has become a life-giving spirit through his triumph over sin and death in the Resurrection. Paul says nothing about the nature of the resurrection body in this text; he speaks of Jesus's spirit as the source of spiritual life, but without reducing Jesus to a spirit.[10]

Q. What else does Paul say about Jesus, Resurrection, and the Spirit?

Paul writes a great deal about those subjects. Here is just one key passage: "If the Spirit of him who raised Jesus from the dead dwells in you, he who raised Christ Jesus from the dead will give life to your mortal bodies also through his Spirit who dwells in you" (Rom 8:11). Thus, Paul

---

[10] For detailed examination of 1 Cor. 15:35–49, see Wright, *The Resurrection of the Son of God*, 340–56.

parallels what the Spirit of God did in raising Jesus from the dead with what he will do to the mortal bodies of Paul's Christian readers. He sees the Spirit as transforming the natural, mortal bodies of believers into resurrection bodies like that of Jesus. When we read this passage in light of 1 Corinthians 15:51–54, where Paul refers to our mortal life being transformed into immortality, it becomes clear that resurrection doesn't mean becoming a spirit but having one's mortal body transformed into a *spiritualized* body, a bodily manner of existing wholly animated by the Spirit of God. This is the same sort of existence the resurrected Jesus has, according to Paul.

Q. How do you explain 1 Peter 3:18, which says Jesus was "put to death in the flesh but made alive in the spirit"? This passage seems to clearly state that the resurrected Jesus is a spirit.

This text is certainly difficult to interpret. It isn't clear whether it refers to the time *between* Jesus's Death and Resurrection, or to the time *after* the Resurrection. In either case, it doesn't mean Jesus is now a *spirit* rather than an embodied being.

If "made alive in the spirit" refers to the time between Jesus's Death and Resurrection, then the text is useless for arguing about the nature of the Resurrection. It would mean that although Jesus's died, he continued to exist in the spirit until the Resurrection. Before his Resurrection he presented his victory over sin. This would mean the passage refers to the so-called descent into hell (in which hell would refer to the state of the dead). According to this view, the text refers to Jesus's visit to abode of the dead, following his Death but before his Resurrection.

Who are the "spirits in prison" (1 Pt 3:19)? Some scholars think this refers to human beings who died in the flood of Noah. Others think it refers to diabolical beings who rebelled against God and who were associated, in Jewish tradition, with the flood. These beings were sometimes represented as residing beneath the earth, where the spirits of the dead were also pictured as residing. In either case, this wouldn't be a reference to the resurrected Jesus "alive in the spirit."

Some scholars don't think 1 Peter 3:18 refers to Jesus's descent into hell, but to a time after his Resurrection, probably his Ascension. According to this view, the "spirits in prison" are fallen angelic beings sometimes thought to reside in the atmosphere. Jesus's Ascension would represent his triumphing over them.

How is it possible to account for Jesus being "made alive in the spirit" without holding that Jesus's Resurrection means he is now a spirit rather than an embodied being? The phrase "made alive in the spirit" certainly doesn't mean made alive *as a spirit*—that is plain on purely linguistic grounds. It appears to mean by means of or through the spirit. If so, the text would mean that Jesus was put to death by means of or through the flesh but that he was made alive by means of or through the Spirit. And by means of or through the Spirit, after his Resurrection, he preached to the spirits in prison, i.e., in the atmosphere, as he ascended to Heaven. It would *not* mean he was a spirit.[11]

---

[11] "*In the flesh . . . in the spirit*: This distinction is not that of 'body' and 'soul' as found in [Greek] philosophy. Thus, 3:19 does not refer to the activity of Christ's 'soul.' The text refers to the two spheres of Christ's existence, that of his earthly life and that of his state as risen Lord transformed by the Spirit (*cf.* Rom 1:3; 1 Cor 15:45; 1 Tim 3:16)." Raymond Edward Brown, *The New Jerome Biblical Commentary* (Englewood Cliffs, NJ: Prentice Hall, 1990), 907.

Q. What are the arguments against the Spiritual Resurrection Theory?

The most obvious argument against the idea of a purely spiritual resurrection is that the Jews of Jesus's day knew nothing of the idea. For them, resurrection referred to what happened to body, not to the spirit. Some Jews rejected the idea of resurrection and of spirits (the Sadducees). Some believed in the resurrection of the body and in spirits (the Pharisees). But, in any case, a spiritual resurrection, if by that one means a resurrection involving no kind of body, would have been regarded as a contradiction in terms.

If Paul and the early Christians wanted only to say that Jesus continued to exist after death as a spirit, it is hard to understand why they would use the term *resurrection*, which would be interpreted as referring to a bodily transformation, rather than a transformation into a spirit. The language of spiritual immortality was common in Judaism of the time.[12] The early Christians knew the difference between a spirit and a spiritual or resurrected body, as seen in Luke 24:39, in which Jesus says, "For a spirit has not flesh and bones as you see that I have."

Which brings us to the point that the earliest accounts of the Resurrection describe it in physical terms—Jesus is not a spirit. Only if these texts are dismissed as later carnalizations of a primitive spiritual experience (as in some versions of the Myth Theory), or radically reinterpreted (as with Jehovah's Witnesses, who claim Jesus only assumed a physical body for a special reason), can we make any sense of the Spiritual Resurrection Theory.

---

[12] Cf. Wis 3:1–4; 4 Mac 18:23; Josephus, *Jewish Wars*, 2.8.11 (154–57); *Antiquities*, 18.1.5 (18).

But, in fact, the case is strong against a carnalizing reinterpretation of radical scholars and the assumed body theory of the Jehovah's Witnesses. The earliest descriptions of Jesus encountered by Paul and the others, as we have seen, have him embodied, not a spirit. The early Christian testimony proclaimed a *bodily* Resurrection. We have no grounds, then, for seeing the gospel accounts as carnalizing reinterpretations. They are consistent with earliest testimony.

As for the *ad hoc* explanation of Jehovah's Witnesses, that Jesus assumed physical bodies for the purpose of appearing to his disciples, the New Testament never refers to Jesus assuming a body of any kind after the Resurrection. On the contrary, the Gospels imply that Jesus's resurrected body is the same body that was crucified and was buried, only now it has been transformed by the power of the Spirit.

Q. What are the key passages of the New Testament that refute the Spiritual Resurrection Theory?

Matthew 28:6. Here, some of Jesus's disciples encounter an angel at the tomb who declares, "He is not here; for he has risen as he said." In other words, Jesus's corpse isn't in the tomb because he has been resurrected. But only if the Resurrection did something to the dead body of Jesus would the angel's comment make sense.

Proponents of the Myth Theory, as noted, claim this account was created much later, as the original understanding of the disciples' experience was replaced by a myth. But most defenders of the Spiritual Resurrection Theory don't have that option. They claim the New Testament supports their view. How, then, do they reply to the angel's comment about the empty tomb?

Jehovah's Witnesses and some others claim that Jesus's body is no longer in the tomb because God disintegrated it. However nowhere does the text state or imply such a thing. The text itself indicates Jesus's body left the tomb when he did—at the Resurrection. Mark 16:6, a parallel account, likewise leaves no room for a disintegrated body.

Luke 24:38. We referenced this text earlier to refute the idea that Jesus was a ghost or spirit. Proponents of the Spiritual Resurrection Theory (especially Jehovah's Witnesses) appeal to the idea of Jesus assuming a body to communicate with his disciples, as noted above. But this argument makes no sense. Why would Jesus assume a body of "flesh and bones," as Jesus himself insists, to convince the disciples he still lived but as a spirit, which is without "flesh and bones"? Jesus's whole point in Luke 24:38 is to show that he is *not* a spirit. For Jesus to appear *as if* he had a body of "flesh and bones" would only mislead or confuse the disciples, if he really were only a spirit after all.

A counter argument is to claim that when Jesus tells his disciples he is not a spirit, he means at that *instance* he is not a spirit, not that in general he is not a spirit. In other words, the disciples think they see a spirit, but Jesus corrects them by telling them that at that moment they're seeing a body of "flesh and bones." But should we suppose Jesus is only quibbling with them about the mode in which he happens to appear in that instance? Is he really saying, "Look, you think I am a spirit right now, but in fact I happen to have assumed a body. You need to get it straight when I am in my usual state as a spirit and when I am visiting you, in which case I assume a body of 'flesh and bones'"? That's rather preposterous.

Defenders of the Spiritual Resurrection Theory sometimes answer that Jesus assumed a "flesh and bones" body so the disciples could see him, much as angels assume bodies so people can see them. There are several points that can be made. First, throughout the Bible angels appear in bodily form, but nowhere are we told that these bodies are "flesh and bones," nor that they are real bodies, as opposed to apparitions of bodies. Second, even assuming that angels are, from time to time, genuinely embodied, their situation is essentially different from Jesus's Resurrection. Angels do not appear in bodily form in order to insist they are *not* spirits, which is what Jesus does in Luke 24:38. Third, are we really supposed to believe that if Jesus wanted to indicate to his disciples that he now lives as a spirit, he couldn't have done so without assuming a body of "flesh and bones"? And why doesn't he say, as we would expect, "Although I appear to you in this form right now, I am really a spirit"?

A more reasonable assumption is that Luke recounts this incident because it counters non-Christian charges that the disciples didn't really encounter the *resurrected* Jesus but saw only a ghost. In other words, Luke opposes a view of Jesus's Resurrection similar to what the proponents of the Spiritual Resurrection Theory hold—namely, Jesus was a spirit.

John 2:19–22. Jesus challenges his enemies: "Destroy this temple, and in three days I will raise it up." According to John, the temple of which Jesus spoke was his body. Later, notes John, the disciples recalled Jesus's statement after the Resurrection. The "it" Jesus promises to raise up is the same body that was crucified, albeit one transformed by the power of the Spirit. If Jesus's corpse had rotted in the grave or disintegrated, then Jesus would not have raised it up, as he said he was going to do.

John 20:24–29. Thomas doubted the Resurrection of Jesus, declaring that unless he saw the marks of the nails in Jesus's hands and touched Jesus's side, he would not believe. Jesus appears to Thomas and shows him his wounds and Thomas apparently touches Jesus. This implies that Jesus's resurrected body was the same body as the one crucified, only it was transformed by the power of the Spirit.

Proponents of the Spiritual Resurrection Theory argue that Jesus merely assumed a physical body here, too, as they claim he did in his appearance to the disciples mentioned in Luke 24:38. Yet why would Jesus assume a body with the marks of his Crucifixion? If this body wasn't the same body that was crucified, then Jesus deceived Thomas by producing a body with wound marks that weren't really wound marks, but only resembled them.

Furthermore, as seen already, it would be absurd for Jesus to assume a physical body in order to prove to the disciples that he had in fact become a spirit. John 20:25–29 makes this view more absurd. It would mean that Jesus assumed a physical body with the marks of his Crucifixion, which would imply that it is the same body as the one crucified, in order to prove he was now a spirit, without the body in which he was crucified.

Acts 2:31. According to Peter, David prophesied Jesus's Resurrection, arguing that God did not permit Jesus's "flesh [to] see corruption." This implies that Jesus's Resurrection body was incorruptible flesh, which contradicts the view that Jesus was a spirit.

Romans 8:11. Paul states that if the Spirit who raised Jesus from the dead dwells in Christians, then God will raise their "mortal bodies also through his Spirit who dwells in" them. On Paul's view, the same body that dies ("mortal bodies") will be raised, even if transformed in the resurrection of the dead, so that it becomes immortal. Since Paul parallels the resurrection of the Christian with the Resurrection of Jesus, we can conclude that the Resurrection of Jesus involved a transformation of his mortal body, not its natural decomposition or disposal by God.

Conclusion: Two Challenges and One Question

For over fifteen years I've led a weekly Bible study at the Byzantine Catholic parish we've attended since shortly after entering the Catholic Church in 1997. Recently, we finished a year-long study of Acts of the Apostles; near the end, I half-jokingly said to the class, "You know, someone needs to write a book titled *Paul: The Apostle of Failure*." It's remarkable how often Paul was dismissed, hounded, hated, stoned, imprisoned, and persecuted. Of course, his message was upsetting and unsettling. It was an all-or-nothing message centered on the Death and Resurrection of Christ—topics which irritated many, to put it mildly. As Paul wrote to the mostly Gentile Christians in Corinth:

> For Jews demand signs and Greeks seek wisdom, but we preach Christ crucified, a stumbling block to Jews and folly to Gentiles, but to those who are called, both Jews and Greeks, Christ the power of God and the wisdom of God. For the foolishness of God is wiser than men, and the weakness of God is stronger than men. (1 Cor 1:22–25)

Paul was a difficult man in many ways, but he was also a brilliant rhetorician and dazzling theologian.[1] Yet he was

---

[1] A good guide to Paul's rhetoric and evangelistic methods is Ben

often rebuffed (sometimes with violence), and the sticking point was, repeatedly, the Resurrection of Christ: "Now when they heard of the resurrection of the dead, some mocked; but others said, 'We will hear you again about this'" (Acts 17:32).

In a real sense, then, things haven't changed for some 2,000 years. The Christian who seeks to evangelize and share the Gospel often finds himself in a strange situation. He might find himself in this sort of conversation with a co-worker or a family member:

> Non-Christian: Hey, it's almost Easter! That means bunnies, eggs, and crazy stories about a man rising from the dead.

> Christian: Um, well, I believe Jesus rose from the dead. There is good historical proof—

> Non-Christian: No offense, but no one can honestly argue that Jesus came back to life.

> Christian: Sure they can. There are plenty of scholars and historians who have shown that—

> Non-Christian: Well, sure, because they're Christian. What else would a Christian say?

> Christian: But there is historical and textual evidence, and there are—

> Non-Christian: You mean the Bible? Sorry, but that's just a bunch of religious propaganda.

In such cases, the Christian can feel as if he has been sent to Circular Christian-Crushing Land, where it is simply

---

Witherington III's *The Acts of the Apostles: A Socio-Rhetorical Commentary* (Grand Rapids, MI: William B. Eerdmans Publishing Company, 1998).

assumed that Christians cannot and do not have any sort of logical, factual legs to stand on. Christians need to provide proof, and when they do it is often dismissed because it is "Christian." People say they want signs and are interested in wisdom, but they sometimes have a funny way of handling what is offered to them. Frankly, it can be discouraging.

So, what to do? First, understand that in a secular world, skepticism cuts both ways. And that, as odd as it might sound, is good news. In other words, while skeptics and secular fundamentalists often act as if their constant appeals to science and reason have adequately explained every aspect of reality, that is only so much "secularist spin,"[2] which actually refuses to think outside its own rather limited, materialist box. In other words, such secularists have simply created a narrative based on their materialist, scientistic assumptions but without actually offering either real proof or satisfying explanations for a whole host of things. Among those is the deep sense of unease and malaise people feel or sense because—to borrow from Walker Percy and Flannery O'Connor—we live in a haunted age. The novelist and essayist Percy, an agnostic as a youth, once wrote of his conversion to Catholicism:

> This life is much too much trouble, far too strange, to arrive at the end of it and then be asked what you make of it and have to answer, "Scientific humanism." That won't do. A poor show. Life is a mystery, love is a delight. Therefore, I take it as axiomatic that one should settle for nothing less than the infinite mystery and infinite delight.[3]

---

[2]   James K. A. Smith, *How (Not) to Be Secular: Reading Charles Taylor* (Grand Rapids, MI: William B. Eerdmans Publishing Company, 2014), 92. Smith's book is a guide to Taylor's lengthy book *A Secular Age* (Cambridge, MA: Harvard University Press, 2007).

[3]   Walker Percy, *Signposts in a Strange Land* (New York: Farrar, Straus

Secular humanism simply does not satisfy hungry souls and searching hearts because it shrinks reality in a way that is unsettling for those who suspect that there really is much more to life than efficient economies, fast food, and faster wi-fi. So, secularism has some explaining to do. And this book has, I think, shown how secularist premises and perspectives have not offered sufficient or compelling explanations for what happened to Jesus of Nazareth, what the Resurrection involved (or didn't involve), and how to account for the radical change in the first Christians and the growth and existence of the Church. To be fair, as we've seen, some scholars with skeptical leanings have spent entire careers trying to offer answers, even if those answers are not always clear or convincing. But some popular atheist writers are, to put it bluntly, either lazy or disingenuous—or both. For example, the Stanford educated atheist Sam Harris dismissively claims there "is no evidence whatsoever, apart from the tendentious writings of the later church, that Jesus ever conceived of himself as anything other than a Jew among Jews, seeking the fulfillment of Judaism—and, likely, the return of Jewish sovereignty in a Roman world."[4] In other words, there was nothing unique about Jesus. "There is nothing to see here," says the smirking atheist—whether of the seventeenth century or the twenty-first century—in front of the empty tomb. "Move along; don't loiter!" He's correct: there is nothing to see in the empty tomb. But he completely misses the pesky fly in his bland secular soup: *Why* is there nothing there? And *why* is the Church still here?

---

and Giroux, 1991), 417.

  [4] Sam Harris, *The End of Faith: Religion, Terror, and the Future of Reason* (New York: W. W. Norton & Company, 2004), 94.

Harris also writes that there "is no reason that our ability to sustain ourselves emotionally and spiritually cannot evolve with technology, politics, and the rest of culture. Indeed, it must evolve, if we are to have any future at all."[5] If that isn't an overt statement of dogmatic faith—in the necessity and inevitability of some sort of evolution—what is? One has to wonder, however, why an appeal to the future is supposed to stir up hope. A future for *what*, exactly? Meanwhile, just like Deepak Chopra, Harris does not address the Resurrection of Christ, and thus evades the central point (though certainly not the only point) of uniqueness that distinguishes Jesus from every other man who has ever lived. Fr. Roch A. Kereszty reminds us,

> No historical person has ever been claimed by his own contemporaries, including his closest disciples and one of his chief enemies, to have been raised back to immortal, divine life in such a way that his appearances changed the disciples' lives and gave rise to a world-wide missionary movement.[6]

Along similar lines, Fr. Gerald O'Collins, who has written several scholarly books on Jesus and the Resurrection, points out that founders of other religious movements—the Siddhartha Gautama (Buddha), Confucius, and Muhammed—had many, many years in which to promote, teach, and spread their beliefs (not to mention, in the case of Islam, wealth and military conquest).

---

5   Ibid., 40.

6   Roch A. Kereszty, O.Cist., *Christianity Among Other Religions: Apologetics in a Contemporary Setting* (Staten Island, NY: St. Pauls, 2006), 138. Kereszty further notes that "the fact that adherents to a strict monotheistic religion such as the faith of Israel would attribute divine status to a crucified human being so shortly after his shameful execution is without parallel in history (*cf.* 1 Cor 16:22; Ph 2:6–11)" (p. 138).

> In the case of Christianity, the founder had none of these advantages: his public career was very short; he lacked military and financial support; and, despite some initial success in attracting followers, at the end he was left alone to face the hostility of both civil and religious authorities.[7]

The new atheists, however, don't address these unsettling questions; much like the old atheists of the seventeenth and eighteenth centuries, they are content to offer vague dismissals or unsatisfying theories.

More and more people, however, are skeptical of secularism, even if they cannot articulate it with any precision; this is what I mean in saying skepticism cuts both ways. Secularism must give an account for why it does not answer the hardest questions and satisfy the deepest thirsts. This, I think, is the biggest reason for the explosion in recent decades in new spiritualities; in many ways, these forms of neo-gnostic and anti-traditional belief systems have paralleled the trajectory of modernity and secularism, like a lost spirit trying to reconnect with a body. These new spiritualities are characterized, in general, by a disregard for history, an emphasis on special knowledge (or *gnosis*), individualism, the spiritualization of science, spiritual evolution, and "religious pluralism as rooted in mystical experience."[8] As the popularity of Spong and Chopra (among many others) indicates, the interpretation given to Jesus by practitioners of the new spirituality movement is appealing to people who wish to be spiritual but not

---

[7]   O'Collins, *Believing in the Resurrection*, Kindle eBook.

[8]   See James A. Herrick's *The Making of the New Spirituality: The Eclipse of the Western Religious Tradition* (Downers Grove, IL: InterVarsity Press, 2003), 33–35. Herrick's excellent book provides both a detailed history and a careful theological examination of the new spirituality movement.

religious, who want to hold on to Jesus but mostly to the parts of Jesus that scratch their metaphysical itch.

A perfect example is the 2014 book *Resurrecting Jesus: Embodying the Spirit of a Revolutionary Mystic* by Adyashanti, an "American-born spiritual teacher devoted to serving the awakening of beings."[9] Whereas Chopra and Spong are often critical, even harshly dismissive, of orthodox Christianity, Adyashanti's tone is calm (befitting a practitioner of Zen Buddhism), accepting, and inclusive. "The Truth I point to is not confined within any religious point of view, belief system, or doctrine," writes Adyashanti, "but is open to all and found within all."[10] Still, there is a clear sense that the likable Adyashanti believes he has inside track on the real Jesus—the "mystical Jesus"—who is so often not really a part of Christianity as it is practiced by most. And he accentuates this with a story of going to a church as a young man and being disappointed by a Catholic priest who "talked about abortion, about how families should be . . . I had a sense that he had *completely* missed the Christian message."[11]

---

[9]   Adyashanti, *Resurrecting Jesus: Embodying the Spirit of a Revolutionary Mystic* (Boulder, CO: Sounds True, 2014), from book's dust jacket.

[10]   Ibid.

[11]   Ibid., 13. The anecdote is interesting since Adyashanti notes how moved he was by the "ritual" and "mystery" he witnessed in seeing people receive Communion. Oddly, he indicates that the homily was after Communion, which is incorrect. The impression given is that Adyashanti was offended that a Catholic priest was presenting Catholic moral teaching to Catholic parishioners instead of articulating mystical theology. He faults the priest for being judgmental (regarding objective truth) while failing to see how judgmental he is of the priest (on decidedly subjective grounds). Adyashanti later writes, "Of course, there are those churches today that are inspired by the real living presence of Christ, but as a whole, Christianity needs new life breathed into it" (p. 24).

In short, Adyashanti takes parts of the "Jesus story"[12] that he likes, largely ignores the historical nature of Christianity, and makes himself the interpreter of Jesus's teachings and life. In his reading, Jesus is a "revolutionary mystic" who "broke down barriers" and helps us "break down the internal walls that separate ourselves from each other, from the world, and from our own divinity."[13] We are told that "divine *being* is what Jesus is here for,"[14] which is a curious statement in light of Paul's teaching that though Christ Jesus "was in the form of God, [he] did not count equality with God a thing to be grasped, but emptied himself, taking the form of a servant, being born in the likeness of men" (Phil 2:5–7). We find, in short, that Jesus is an enlightened man who enters into divinity by realizing that divinity is within him; the key is to "step through the veil and enter into the spiritual domain."[15] The name for this step, Adyashanti says, is "repent."[16] The key moments in Jesus's life—the temptation, the transfiguration, the trial, the Crucifixion—are all meant to be understood "mythically, not historically or factually"; they are "archetypes of the spiritual journey."[17]

And what of Jesus's Resurrection? There is mention of "'great transcendence' and 'a new orientation'" and "great release" and "awakening"[18] and "the death of self."[19] All that is left is "a selfless and benevolent presence"[20] and a "great heart-

---

12 Ibid., xiii.
13 Ibid., 16–17.
14 Ibid., 18.
15 Ibid., 62.
16 Ibid.
17 Ibid., 168.
18 Ibid., 191.
19 Ibid., 192.
20 Ibid., 192.

fulness, a great sense of compassion for the world."[21] While Adyashanti avoids terms such as nirvana, he indicates that there is a cessation of desire, which is the goal of Buddhism.

There are three essential characteristics of Adyashanti's presentation that cannot be reconciled with orthodox Christianity, each of which touches on important points made throughout this book.

The first is that God is not other and personal, but is essentially an impersonal, monistic Force. He is not Creator, nor is he the End of all things; he is not Alpha and Omega. As in most of the new spiritualities, God is the Impersonal Everything; we are God if only we will realize it. That is enlightenment, which is sometimes described as "Christ consciousness." In Christianity, since God is personal and Creator, the free-willed rupture of communion with God is a renunciation of love and life; sin is the choice of oneself over God. But for Adyashanti the greatest failing we can have is to not recognize that we are divine and embrace it. Whereas in the Judeo-Christian tradition God always initiates and offers salvation, in the new spiritualities man initiates and creates enlightenment. In Christianity, the Father reveals his love for his creation and creatures by sending his Son, who becomes man in order to demonstrate love, which is most perfectly revealed on the Cross: "Greater love has no man than this, that a man lay down his life for his friends" (Jn 15:13). The Crucifixion is the demonstration of perfect love, and the Resurrection is validation of perfect love. However, for Adyashanti, Jesus did not die for you and me; no, Jesus "cared so much that he completely gave himself to life in order to

---

[21] Ibid., 193.

redeem it."[22] Redemption, then, is not about recovered communion with the Lord and Giver of Life, but achieving a state of detached autonomy.

Secondly, Adyashanti (like almost all new spirituality teachers) presents Jesus as an archetype, a wonderful guru-like avatar who shows us what we can do if only we see the "spark of divinity" and grasp "the ray of divinity"[23] set before us. The humanity of Jesus is not significant; the uniqueness of Jesus of Nazareth, the Incarnate Word of God, is watered down and poured down the drain of mythological or mystical interpretations.[24] Jesus did not come, then, to bridge the chasm between man and God, but to realize his own divinity. This, of course, is an inversion of what orthodox Christianity teaches, for throughout the Gospels Jesus indicates and describes his perfect and unique relationship with the Father—a relationship he desires his disciples to enter into: "I in them and you in me, that they may become perfectly one, so that the world may know that you have sent me and have loved them even as you have loved me" (Jn 17:23). And that relationship, in the Christian tradition, is called many things: *koinonia*, communion, *theosis*, deification, and partaking in the divine nature.[25] The key here is that it is only possible because of the

---

22   Ibid., 230.

23   Ibid., 227.

24   Herrick notes that Christians argue "that history provides their perspective with an objective foundation that serves to ground spiritual claims in verifiable events" while new spirituality proponents move "away from history and toward myth, away from physical events and toward transcendent symbols, away from verifiable occurrences and toward imaginative narratives" (*The Making of the New Spirituality: The Eclipse of the Western Religious Tradition*, 255).

25   See Fr. David Vincent Meconi and Carl E. Olson, eds., *Called to Be the Children of God: The Catholic Theology of Human Deification* (San Francisco: Ignatius Press, 2016).

work of Christ and the power of the Holy Spirit; it is a free gift by which we become children of God through the grace of God (*cf.* 1 Jn 3:1): "We were buried therefore with him by baptism into death, so that as Christ was raised from the dead by the glory of the Father, we too might walk in newness of life" (Rom 6:4). The Resurrection is not a mythological or archetypical story but the conquering of death by death.

Third, we can begin to see how much secular fundamentalism and the new spiritualities actually share, in both premises and perspectives. Both are man-centered; both emphasize the autonomy of man and his ability to supposedly save himself. Put another way, both belief systems refuse to admit their reliance on God and refuse to bow before him. The great Orthodox theologian Fr. Alexander Schmemann, in *For the Life of the World*, wrote that most people have missed the essential core—or grave defect—of secularism. "Secularism, I submit, is above all a negation of worship. . . . If secularism in theological terms is a heresy, it is primarily a heresy about man. It is the negation of man as a worshiping being."[26] Fr. Schmemann pointed out that secularism is not the same as atheism; in fact, secularism does not try to eliminate God as much as completely change man's relationship with God. Put very simply, God becomes a commodity—an idea, a symbol, a security blanket—for our use. Man was made to adore, but has chosen to be autonomous. And now man is haunted, trapped in his secularist cage—or, in the case of many others, his spiritual-but-not-religious box. Neither the skeptic nor the Zen master is interested in worshiping God; neither thinks it is necessary to fall in awe and wonder before

---

[26] Alexander Schmemann, *For the Life of the World: Sacraments and Orthodoxy* (St. Vladimir's Seminary Press, 1973), 118.

the crucified One and exclaim, "Worthy is the Lamb who was slain, to receive power and wealth and wisdom and might and honor and glory and blessing!" (Rev 5:12).

The deepest challenge of the Resurrection of Jesus Christ is that it reiterates dramatically and insistently the question asked of the disciples as they gazed upon pagan shrines cut into the rocks at Caesarea Philippi—"But who do you say that I am?" (Mk 8:29; Mt 16:15; Lk 9:20)—and demands an answer. An *answer*. Not a theory; not a guess; not a personal reflection; not an extended exegetical discourse. No, an answer:

> Now Thomas, one of the twelve, called the Twin, was not with them when Jesus came. So the other disciples told him, "We have seen the Lord." But he said to them, "Unless I see in his hands the print of the nails, and place my finger in the mark of the nails, and place my hand in his side, I will not believe."
>
> Eight days later, his disciples were again in the house, and Thomas was with them. The doors were shut, but Jesus came and stood among them, and said, "Peace be with you." Then he said to Thomas, "Put your finger here, and see my hands; and put out your hand, and place it in my side; do not be faithless, but believing." Thomas answered him, "My Lord and my God!" Jesus said to him, "Have you believed because you have seen me? Blessed are those who have not seen and yet believe."
>
> Now Jesus did many other signs in the presence of the disciples, which are not written in this book; but these are written that you may believe that Jesus is the Christ, the Son of God, and that believing you may have life in his name. (Jn 20:24–31)

Bibliography

Adam, Karl. *The Christ of Faith*. New York: Pantheon Books, 1957.

———. *The Son of God*. London: Sheed & Ward, 1937.

Adyashanti. *Resurrecting Jesus: Embodying the Spirit of a Revolutionary Mystic*. Boulder, CO: Sounds True, 2014.

Allen, Charlotte. *The Human Christ: The Search for the Historical Jesus*. New York: The Free Press, 1998.

Allison, Dale C. *Jesus of Nazareth: Millenarian Prophet*. Minneapolis, MN: Fortress Press, 1998.

Aslan, Reza. *Zealot: The Life and Times of Jesus of Nazareth*. New York: Random House, 2013.

Baker, Kenneth. *Jesus Christ—True God and True Man: A Handbook of Christology for Non-Theologians*. South Bend, IN: St. Augustine's Press, 2013.

Barnett, Paul. *Is the New Testament Reliable?* Downers Grove, IL: InterVarsity Press, 2003.

Bauckham, Richard. *Jesus and the Eyewitnesses: The Gospels As Eyewitness Testimony*. Grand Rapids, MI: William B. Eerdmans Publishing Company, 2006.

Beckwith, Francis J., William Lane Craig, and J.P. Moreland, eds. *To Everyone an Answer: A Case for the Christian Worldview*: Downers Grove, IL: InterVarsity Press, 2004.

Beilby, James K., and Paul Rhodes Eddy. *The Historical Jesus: Five Views*. Downers Grove, IL: IVP Academic, 2009.

Benedict XVI. *Jesus of Nazareth: From the Baptism in the Jordan to the Transfiguration*. New York: Doubleday, 2007.

———. *Jesus of Nazareth—Holy Week: From the Entrance into Jerusalem to the Resurrection*. San Francisco: Ignatius Press, 2011.

Bird, Michael, Craig A. Evans, Simon J. Gathercole, Charles E. Hill, and Chris Tilling. *How God Became Man: The Real Origins of Belief in Jesus' Divine Nature*. Grand Rapids, MI: Zondervan, 2014.

Blomberg, Craig L. *The Historical Reliability of the Gospels*. Second Edition. Grand Rapids, MI: IVP Academic, 2007.

———. *Making Sense of the New Testament: Three Crucial Questions*. Grand Rapids, MI: Baker Academic, 2004.

Bock, Darrell L. *Studying the Historical Jesus: A Guide to Sources and Methods*. Grand Rapids, MI: Baker Academic, 2002.

Bock, Darrell, L., and Herrick, Gregory J. *Jesus in Context: Background Readings for Gospel Study*. Grand Rapids, MI: Baker Academic, 2005.

Bockmuehl, Markus, ed. *The Cambridge Companion to Jesus*. New York: Cambridge University Press, 2001.

Borg, Marcus J., and N. T. Wright. *The Meaning of Jesus: Two Visions*. San Francisco: HarperSanFrancisco, 1999.

Bouyer, Louis. *The Eternal Son: A Theology of the Word of God and Christology*. Huntington, IN: Our Sunday Visitor, 1978.

Boyd, Gregory A., and Paul Rhodes Eddy. *Lord or Legend: Wrestling with the Jesus Dilemma*. Grand Rapids, MI: BakerBooks, 2007.

Brown, Raymond E. *The Virginal Conception and Bodily Resurrection of Jesus.* New York: Paulist Press, 1973.

Bruce, F. F. *The New Testament Documents: Are They Reliable?* Downers Grove, IL: InterVarsity Press, 1972.

Cerfaux, Lucien. *The Christian in the Theology of St. Paul.* New York: Herder and Herder, 1967.

———. *The Spiritual Journey of Saint Paul.* New York: Sheed and Ward, 1968.

Copan, Paul, ed. *Will the Real Jesus Please Stand Up? A Debate Between William Lane Craig and John Dominic Crossan.* Grand Rapids, MI: Baker Books, 1998.

Craig, William Lane. *Reasonable Faith: Christian Truth and Apologetics.* Wheaton, IL: Crossway Books, 1994.

———. *The Son Rises: The Historical Evidence for the Resurrection of Jesus.* Eugene, OR: Wipf and Stock Publishers, 2000.

Crossan, John Dominic. *The Birth of Christianity: Discovering What Happened in the Years Immediately After the Execution of Jesus.* San Francisco: HarperSanFrancisco, 1997.

———. *The Historical Jesus: The Life of a Mediterranean Jewish Peasant.* San Francisco: HarperSanFrancisco, 1992.

———. *Jesus: A Revolutionary Biography.* San Francisco: HarperSanFrancisco, 1994.

Cummings, Owen F. *Coming to Christ: A Study in Christian Eschatology.* New York: University Press of America, 1998.

Daley, Brian E. *The Hope of the Early Church: A Handbook of Patristic Eschatology.* Grand Rapids, MI: Baker Academic, 2010.

Daniélou, Jean. *Christ and Us.* New York: Sheed and Ward, 1961.

Davis, Stephen T. *Risen Indeed: Making Sense of the Resurrection.* Grand Rapids, MI: William B. Eerdmans Publishing Company, 1993.

Davis, Stephen T., Daniel Kendall, and Gerald O'Collins, eds. *The Resurrection.* New York: Oxford University Press, 1998.

Dulles, Avery. *Apologetics and the Biblical Christ.* Westminster, MD: The Newman Press, 1964.

———. *A History of Apologetics.* San Francisco: Ignatius Press, 2005.

Eddy, Paul Rhodes, and Gregory A. Boyd. *The Jesus Legend: A Case for the Historical Reliability of the Synoptic Jesus Tradition.* Grand Rapids, MI: Baker Academic, 2007.

Evans, C. Stephen. *The Historical Christ and the Jesus of Faith: The Incarnational Narrative as History.* Oxford: Clarendon Press, 1996.

Evans, Craig A. *Fabricating Jesus: How Modern Scholars Distort the Gospels.* Downers Grove, IL: InterVarsity Press, 2006.

———. *From Jesus to the Church: The First Christian Generation.* Louisville, KY: Westminster John Knox Press, 2014.

Flew, Anthony, and Gary Habermas. *Did the Resurrection Happen? A Conversation with Gary Habermas and Antony Flew.* Edited by David Baggett. Downers Grove, IL: InterVarsity Press, 2009.

Fredricksen, Paula. *From Jesus to Christ: The Origins of the New Testament Images of Jesus.* New Haven, CT: Yale University Press, 2000.

Funk, Robert W. *Honest to Jesus: Jesus for a New Millennium.* San Francisco: HarperSanFrancisco, 1996.

Geisler, Norman L. *The Battle for the Resurrection*. Nashville, TN: Thomas Nelson Publishers, 1992.

Grant, Michael. *Jesus: An Historian's Review of the Gospels*. New York: Charles Scribner's Sons, 1977.

Groothuis, Douglas. *Christian Apologetics: A Comprehensive Case for Biblical Faith*. Downers Grove, IL: IVP Academic, 2011.

Guardini, Romano. *The Lord*. Washington, D.C.: Regnery Gateway, 1988.

Guitton, Jean. *The Problem of Jesus: A Free-Thinker's Diary*. New York: P.J. Kenedy & Sons, 1955.

Habermas, Gary R., and Michael R. Licona. *The Case for the Resurrection of Jesus*. Grand Rapids, MI: Kregel Publications, 2004.

Harris, Sam. *The End of Faith: Religion, Terror, and the Future of Reason*. New York: W. W. Norton & Company, 2004.

Heaney, John J., ed. *Faith, Reason, and the Gospels: A Magnificent Summary of Modern Thought on a Vital Question*. Westminster, MD: The Newman Press, 1961.

Hengel, Martin. *Between Jesus and Paul*. Minneapolis, MN: Fortress Press, 1983.

Hengel, Martin, and Anna Maria Schwemer. *Paul Between Damascus and Antioch: The Unknown Years*. Louisville, KY: Westminster John Knox Press, 1997.

Herrick, James A. *The Making of the New Spirituality: The Eclipse of the Western Religious Tradition*. Downers Grove, IL: InterVarsity Press, 2003.

Hitchens, Christopher. *God Is Not Great: How Religion Poisons Everything*. New York: Twelve, 2007.

Hutchinson, Robert J. *Searching For Jesus: New Discoveries in the Quest for Jesus of Nazareth—And How They Confirm the Gospel Accounts.* Nashville, TN: Nelson Books, 2015.

Jones, Timothy Paul. *Misquoting Truth: A Guide to the Fallacies of Bart Ehrman's Misquoting Jesus.* Downers Grove, IL: InterVarsity Press, 2007.

Keener, Craig S. *The IVP Bible Background Commentary: New Testament.* Downers Grove, IL: IVP Academic, 1993.

———. *The Historical Jesus of the Gospels.* Grand Rapids, MI: William B. Eerdmans Publishing Company, 2009.

Kelly, J. N. D. *Early Christian Doctrines.* New York: Harper & Row, Publishers, 1960.

Kereszty, Roch A. *Christianity Among Other Religions: Apologetics in a Contemporary Context.* Staten Island, NY: St. Pauls, 2006.

———. *Jesus Christ: Fundamentals of Christology.* Staten Island, NY: St. Pauls, 2002.

Komoszewski, J. Ed, M. James Sawyer, and Daniel B. Wallace. *Reinventing Jesus: How Contemporary Skeptics Miss the Real Jesus and Mislead Popular Culture.* Grand Rapids, MI: Kregel Publications, 2006.

Kreeft, Peter J., and Ronald K. Tacelli. *Handbook of Catholic Apologetics: Reasoned Answers to Questions of Faith.* San Francisco: Ignatius Press, 2009.

Léon-Dufour, Xavier. *Resurrection and the Easter Message.* New York: Hold, Rinehart and Winston, 1971.

Licona, Michael R. *The Resurrection of Jesus: A New Historiographical Approach.* Downers Grove, IL: InterVarsity Press, 2010.

Lohfink, Gerhard. *Jesus of Nazareth: What He Wanted, Who He Was.* Collegeville, MN: Liturgical Press, 2012.

———. *No Irrelevant Jesus: On Jesus and the Church Today.* Collegeville, MN: Liturgical Press, 2014.

Marxsen, Willi. *The Resurrection of Jesus of Nazareth.* Philadelphia: Fortress Press, 1970.

Meier, John P. *A Marginal Jew: Rethinking the Historical Jesus.* New York: Doubleday, 1991.

Metzger, Bruce M. *The New Testament: Its Background, Growth, and Content.* New York: Abingdon Press, 1965.

O'Collins, Gerald. *Believing in the Resurrection: The Meaning and Promise of the Risen Jesus.* New York: Paulist Press, 2012.

———. *Christology: A Biblical, Historical, and Systematic Study of Jesus.* New York: Oxford University Press, 1995.

———. *Jesus Our Redeemer: A Christian Approach to Salvation.* New York: Oxford University Press, 2007.

O'Collins, Gerald, and Daniel Kendall. *Focus on Jesus: Essays on Christology and Soteriology.* Herefordshire: Gracewing, 1996.

Pitre, Brant. *The Case for Jesus: The Biblical and Historical Evidence for Christ.* New York: Image, 2016.

———. *Jesus and the Last Supper.* Grand Rapids, MI: William B. Eerdmans Publishing Company, 2015.

Purtill, Richard. *Reason to Believe: Why Faith Makes Sense.* San Francisco: Ignatius Press, 2009.

Sanders, E. P. *The Historical Figure of Jesus.* London: The Penguin Press, 1993.

Schönborn, Christoph Cardinal. *God Sent His Son: A Contemporary Christology.* San Francisco: Ignatius Press, 2010.

Schonfield, Hugh J. *The Passover Plot: A New Interpretation of the Life and Death of Jesus*. New York: Bantam Books, 1969.

Spong, John Shelby. *Liberating the Gospels? Reading the Bible with Jewish Eyes*. San Francisco: HarperSanFrancisco, 1996.

———. *A New Christianity for a New World: Why Traditional Faith Is Dying and How a New Faith Is Being Born*. San Francisco: HarperSanFrancisco, 2001.

———. *Why Christianity Must Change or Die: A Bishop Speaks to Believers in Exile*. San Francisco: HarperSanFrancisco, 1998.

Sri, Edward. *Love Unveiled: The Catholic Faith Explained*. San Francisco: Ignatius Press, 2015.

Stanton, Graham. *Gospel Truth? New Light on Jesus and the Gospels*. Valley Forge, PA: Trinity Press International, 1995.

Van Voorst, Robert E. *Jesus Outside the New Testament: An Introduction to the Ancient Evidence*. Grand Rapids, MI: William B. Eerdmans Publishing Company, 2000.

Vermes, Geza. *The Authentic Gospel of Jesus*. New York: Penguin Books, 2003.

———. *The Changing Faces of Jesus*. New York: Viking Compass, 2001.

Weaver, Walter P. *The Historical Jesus in the Twentieth Century: 1900–1950*. Harrisburg, PA: Trinity Press International, 1999.

Wenham, David. *Paul: Follower of Jesus or Founder of Christianity?* Grand Rapids, MI: William B. Eerdmans Publishing Company, 1995.

Wilkins, Michael J., and J. P. Moreland. *Jesus Under Fire: Modern Scholarship Reinvents the Historical Jesus.* Grand Rapids, MI: Zondervan, 1995.

Wills, Garry. *What Jesus Meant.* New York: Viking, 2006.

Witherington III, Ben. *The Jesus Quest: The Third Search for the Jew of Nazareth.* Downers Grove, IL: InterVarsity Press, 1997.

———. *The Paul Quest: The Renewed Search for the Jew of Tarsus.* Downers Grove, IL: InterVarsity Press, 1998.

Wright, N. T. *The Challenge of Jesus: Rediscovering Who Jesus Was and Is.* Downers Grove, IL: InterVarsity Press, 1999.

———. *Jesus and the Victory of God.* Minneapolis, MN: Fortress Press, 1996.

———. *The New Testament and the People of God.* Minneapolis, MN: Fortress Press, 1992.

———. *The Resurrection and the Son of God.* Minneapolis, MN: Fortress Press, 2003.

———. *What Saint Paul Really Said: Was Paul of Tarsus the Real Founder of Christianity?* Grand Rapids, MI: William B. Eerdmans Publishing Company, 1997.

———. *Who Was Jesus?* Grand Rapids, MI: William B. Eerdmans Publishing Company, 1992.